Isabel,
May you continue to be a
model of strength, truth,
and clarity.

Pete Reiely

A PATH WITH HEART

A PATH
WITH
HEART

THE INNER JOURNEY TO
TEACHING MASTERY

PETE REILLY

IRIMI HORIZONS

ISBN 978-0-9861354-0-8

Irimi Horizons Publishing
Tomkins Cove, NY 10986
www.apathwithheart.net
www.preilly.wordpress.org

David Whyte, "Start Close In" from *River Flow: New & Selected Poems*, www.davidwhyte.
com. Printed with permission from Many Rivers Press, © Many Rivers Press, Langley,
Washington.

William Stafford, "The Way It Is" from *Ask Me: 100 Essential Poems*. Copyright
© 1998 by the Estate of William Stafford. Reprinted with the permission of The
Permissions Company, Inc. on behalf of Graywolf Press, Minneapolis, Minnesota, www.
graywolfpress.org.

Portia Nelson, "Autobiography in Five Short Chapters" from *There's a Hole In My
Sidewalk: The Romance of Self Discovery*. Reprinted with the permission of Beyond
Words/Atria, a division of Simon and Schuster, Inc. Copyright © 1993 by Portia Nelson.
All Rights Reserved.

Charles Bukowski, "The Laughing Heart" from *Betting on the Muse: Poems & Stories* by
Charles Bukowski. Copyright © 1996 by Linda Lee Bukowski. Reprinted by permission
of Harper Collins Publishers.

Book design by Tom McKeveny

Contents

To the many teachers who

have touched my life both in

and out of the classroom...and

to my family, who has loved me

every step of the way, always

teaching me what it is

to be truly human.

Introduction

I began my teaching career four decades ago, in a small town in the Adirondack mountains of upstate New York. It was a relatively poor, working-class town whose principal industry was logging. The winters were long, but the town was situated on a beautiful lake at the foot of a wonderful ski slope. In winter the students skied, rode snowmobiles, ice-fished, hunted, and trapped, and in summer they swam, fished, and boated. Despite pockets of poverty, as well as a lack of jobs and opportunity, it was a great place for a kid to grow up.

I began teaching midyear, just after the Christmas holidays. The first-year English teacher who began the semester was quitting and I was to take the reins for the rest of the year. The principal, Mr. LeBarge, asked me to observe Miss Greco for a week before she left, and I remember her standing in the hall sobbing as classes changed. "Don't let them do this to you, Pete!" she sputtered through her tears.

I was all of twenty-three, six foot five, a star Division III basketball player with a great student teaching experience under my belt. As I listened to her I thought, "Are you kidding? There's no way that these middle and high school kids will ever get to me!"

How wrong I was. No matter what I tried, no matter how hard I worked, when the class was turned over to me it became a total nightmare. My size, my basketball career, my student teaching, and my cocky self-confidence—none of these made any difference to the students, and I began suffering the fate of many first-year teachers who lose control of their classes. It was very painful and it made me question whether I was cut out to be a teacher, *and* whether I would come back the following year. My confidence in myself hit an all-time low.

Thankfully, I survived, and I came back. The next ten years were ten of the most meaningful of my life. I met Liz (a first-year math teacher), who would later become my wife; I was introduced to the first personal computers and the power of technology; I became the varsity basketball coach; I learned how to ski. But what made this part of my career so profound were my students. They turned my world upside down and, strange as it might seem, taught me as much as I taught them. The mirror they provided was both an invitation for me to self-reflect and a call to wake up and become more self-aware. They reflected back to me my strengths and my weaknesses; and over the years, with their help, I began to change, as a teacher and as a person.

The longer I taught, the more clearly I began to see that my professional transformation and my personal transformation were one and the same. As I became more present, open, and connected to my students, I found that I was also becoming more present, open, and connected outside the classroom. My students taught me that I was the "living curriculum" and that who I was, and how I behaved, had an enormous impact on them as students and as human beings.

What else did I learn? Many things, but perhaps the most important lesson they taught me was the limits of power; for no matter how hard

I worked; no matter how creative, engaging, or entertaining I was; no matter my logic, my authority as teacher, or any positive or negative incentive I could create to motivate them—I could not force a single student to learn a single thing...unless he or she willingly chose to do so.

For me, this lesson was profound. It forced me to look beyond myself, my agenda, and what "I" wanted. It was obvious that in order to be a great teacher I needed to build relationships and trust; I needed to inspire and motivate; I needed to understand my students before I could expect to be understood; I needed to be more present, open, and connected to their needs, their lives, their dreams.

In essence, I was being taught to cultivate a set of personal attributes and a classroom presence that, when combined with my subject matter knowledge and the appropriate pedagogy, would lead my students to *willingly* put in the effort needed to achieve their best academically, as well as to bring forth their gifts, their curiosity, their innate passion for learning.

So, I began my path to mastery. But how shall we define Teaching Mastery? It might be helpful to examine the definition offered by the New York State Master Teacher Program (NYSMTP), in partnership with the State University of New York and with Math for America.[1]

What Defines a Master Teacher?

Three areas of ability and commitment to growth are essential to successful participation in the Master Teacher community: content knowledge, pedagogy, and a deep understanding of students. Master Teachers are strong classroom teachers with clear goals for further developing their breadth and depth in all these areas:

1. **Knowledge of content:** Master Teachers have been exposed to and grappled with ideas that are central to their

discipline at advanced levels. Like any professionals in STEM (science, technology, engineering, and math), however, they view their knowledge as incomplete.

2. **Knowledge of pedagogy:** Master Teachers have developed a deep understanding of professional knowledge for teaching, and they strive to incorporate successful practices in their work. They continually evaluate, refine, and adapt their practice to better meet the needs of their students.

3. **Knowledge of students:** Master Teachers possess an extensive knowledge of their students' neighborhoods, cultures, and values. Master Teachers see students' families and community as resources in their efforts to inspire them to study STEM disciplines.

To this list I invite you to consider adding:

4. **Knowledge of self:** Master Teachers understand that their personality and classroom presence have a major impact on student learning; consequently they practice self-reflection and self-awareness. They acknowledge and embrace their gifts and strengths (as well as those of their students), and they work to minimize lifelong personal habits and patterns of behavior that may inhibit their effectiveness. Master Teachers engage in deliberate practices to cultivate the personal attributes necessary for building positive teacher-student relationships, as well as a "self" that is authentic, fully present, and centered. They maintain strong connections to their purpose and calling, and a passion for their students' success, their subject matter, and their profession.

Unfortunately, many well-intentioned, mainstream educational organizations and initiatives, like the New York State Master Teacher Program, tend to ignore the importance of the personal attributes and classroom presence (the "self") of the teacher who is operating at the heart of the teaching and learning process.

Experience tells us that teachers can have a deep **knowledge of content, pedagogy**, and their **students** and yet not be considered Master Teachers. For example, a teacher who has any of the personality traits listed below is likely to experience only limited success in the classroom:

Overly structured and uncomfortable without a script

Needs to be the center of attention

Quick to anger

Easily overwhelmed

Isn't resilient and whose passion is waning

Difficulty with accountability and blames the kids

Low self-esteem and low expectations

Little confidence and risk averse

Uncomfortable with intimacy

Difficulty listening

Scattered and unorganized

By the way, because we're human beings, no one is excluded from the "gifts and flaws" club. We all have them, whether we're aware of them or not. What makes Master Teachers different is that they deliberately seek to reflect and become more self-aware. They teach from the inside out and engage in practices that minimize the personal attributes that may be impeding student learning, while simultaneously they cultivate the gifts and strengths that enhance it.

So, it's left to each of us to find a path to personal and professional self-awareness, and to Teaching Mastery, that is right for us. This book both invites you on the journey and attempts to provide a few landmarks to guide you, the traveler.

Few shortcuts exist for mastery of any sort, but especially Teaching Mastery. Believe me, I'd love to write a book called *The Top 10 Tips to Becoming a Master Teacher*, have us all take a test on the material, get the certification, buy the T-shirt, and step into the classroom as newly minted Master Teachers! But we know in our hearts that studying the "Top 10 Tips" won't produce mastery any more than reading about or watching someone play the piano will make us keyboard virtuosos.

It may help to think of mastery as a lifelong journey, not an end state. Thinking of Teaching Mastery this way makes it easier to commit to the rigors of deliberate practice, ongoing reflection, and continuous learning. For it's only through engaging in the perpetual cycle of practice, reflection, and feedback that we can hope to cultivate our best and most effective "self"...a self that at its core is meant to serve others—our students.

In my experience human beings have shown themselves to be resilient, self-healing, self-learning organisms; and when we as educators turn our attention inward, when we're able to find the wisdom within us, we find the path that is precisely right for us, and us alone.

It's my hope that this book will broaden the conversation about great teaching and help you navigate your own path to Teaching Mastery.

Harvest Home

In the ideal

our classrooms fill, like cornucopia,

overflowing with the bounty of our grange.

Life stories heaped among the texts

spill into the hallways of our schools,

crowd the sidewalks or the subways

or ride yellow buses home,

altering the form of knowing,

changing heads,

changing hearts,

changing history,

bringing harvest home.

—BETTYE T. SPINNER

CHAPTER 1

THE INNER PATH

Ask yourself and yourself alone one question. It is this: does this path have a heart? All paths are the same. They are paths going through the brush or into the brush or under the brush. Does this path have a heart is the only question. If it does, then the path is good. If it doesn't, then it is of no use.

—Carlos Castaneda

A Path

When you chose to become a teacher, you chose a "calling," a "path with heart," because teaching is an invitation to a world of possibility...for your students and also, if you're open to it, for yourself. It's by turning your own promise into practice that you're able to unlock the potential of your students and make a difference in the world, for teaching is about big things, not little.

Though it may sound strange, it's no less true that who you are, your personality, and your character all lie at the root of good teaching.

This book is an invitation to explore teaching, especially Teaching Mastery, as a journey of personal self-discovery—a path of the heart. It challenges you to look at "soft skills" as "essential skills" and at personal development as an important component of professional development, part of the path to professional mastery.

No matter how we define effectiveness, there is a growing body of research indicating that teaching involves a complex set of knowledge, abilities, and personal attributes in dynamic interplay...**most of what makes a teacher effective is his or her "soft skills" and personal attributes.**

—The National Council on Teacher Quality[1]

This personal approach to teaching and learning, and its focus on you the teacher and you the human being, is exactly what's needed to help meet the call for higher levels of student achievement, while maintaining the classroom as a place of personal discovery and professional growth. Unfortunately, it's rare to find professional development and teacher preparation programs that *focus on the inner life, emotional well-being, and classroom presence of the teacher.*

Most professional development and teacher preparation programs focus on the external elements of teaching: curriculum, pedagogy, and technology, to name a few. Rarely, if ever, do they focus on the human beings—the teachers—who are tasked with implementing them.

While training in the external elements of the educational environment (knowledge and skills) is vital, research clearly indicates that focusing on the more-complex aspects of teaching—attitude, self-awareness, authenticity, and trust, as well as conquering rising levels of personal and professional stress—are key components of classroom success. Bringing our "best" and most effective "self" to the classroom benefits us and our students, because it's by taking care of ourselves (in mind, body, and heart), in service to a larger purpose, that we're best able to be present, open, and connected to them. As Parker Palmer says,

You teach who you are.[2]

A Calling

Most of us are born with hearts that yearn for meaning. We want our lives to count for something, and we hope that our daily work will provide us with a life as well as a living. The classic story of three stonecut-ters helps us see that the true impact of our work goes far beyond the day-to-day tasks that consume so much of our time and energy.

> A traveler came across three stonecutters working in a quarry. Each was chipping away at separate blocks of stone. Curious, he asked the first stonecutter what he was doing. "What? Are you blind?" the stonecutter shouted. "Can't you see I'm cutting this stupid piece of stone?"
>
> The man walked to the second stonecutter, who seemed a little happier, and asked him the same question. The stone-cutter replied, "I'm cutting this block of stone so that the mason can build a straight wall."
>
> Finally, he approached the third stonecutter, who seemed to be the happiest of the three, and asked him what he was doing. "I'm building a cathedral," he replied with a smile.

Like the third stonecutter, knowing that the work we do as teachers can make a positive impact on a child's life—and sometimes, through that child, an impact as well on the world writ large—makes our personal sacrifices and toil worthwhile. As educators, we have the opportunity to build cathedrals of knowledge and opportunity, not merely chip away at stones.

So Many Challenges

While we may have entered teaching to be in service to others, and to contribute to a purpose larger than ourselves, the current landscape of deep educational budget cuts, teacher layoffs, larger class sizes, and de-creasing resources probably makes it especially challenging to maintain our sense of optimism, purpose, and heart.

To make matters worse, at the same time many school districts are downsizing their educational workforce, they're adding the demands of high-stakes testing via the Common Core Curriculum,[3] new professional evaluation processes, more mainstreamed students, much more paperwork, angrier parents, and advanced professional development with initiatives ranging from antibullying to new technology. Of course, while all this is happening we're still expected to provide a safe, individualized, nurturing environment for every student, and higher achievement scores.

Stress levels in the classroom are at an all-time high. Even the best teachers in the best schools are feeling the weight of an educational environment that is permeated by a culture of scarcity, a fear-based system of accountability, sometimes union demonizing, and frequent teacher bashing. Add a growing number of students with emotional, language, and behavioral challenges and it isn't hard to see why nearly 50 percent of teachers leave the field within their first five years.[4] You can hear the fear and anxiety in the words of one teacher who describes her frustration this way:

> I'm trying to get through this lesson so my kids will do well on the standardized tests and I'll be able to keep my job. But my students aren't paying attention and don't care a hoot about this test. —A teacher (in the program of Cultivating Awareness and Resilience in Education)[5]

As in any profession, there are plenty of operational details in teaching that need attention. There are lesson plans to write, activities to develop, grades to analyze, meetings to attend, new technology to learn, kids to monitor, parents to contact, new programs to be implemented... the list seems endless. As more of our time as teachers is devoured by the details of our jobs, it gets easier to let our underlying purpose—the "big picture"—drift further into the background, until at last we become disconnected from it.

One day leads drearily to the next, even as we deal with the overwhelming urgency of the moment. We may lose sight of the horizon and go through the day with eyes cast down, and when we happen to look up, we can't "see the forest for the trees."

In short, we're lost.

John, a 12th grade physics teacher, remembers:

> I was so consumed by the need for my students to pass the [New York State] Regents [test] that one day I was asked a question by a very earnest student, and responded: "That's a great question; but we don't have time for it today." After class, I wondered: how had I gotten so disconnected from my students, so wrapped up in my lesson plan, that I was ignoring legitimate questions? I might as well have hung a neon sign around my neck saying, "Don't Bother Me—I don't have time for you!" It was a terrible response and an awful wake-up call. I was no longer the teacher I wanted to be.

Administrators feel the pressure, too. Some 89% feel overwhelmed by the tasks on their plates, 80% scold themselves when they perform less than perfectly, while 84% neglect to take care of themselves in the midst of stress. The National Commission on Teaching and America's Future (2007) estimates that attrition costs U.S. public schools more than $7 billion per year.[6]

As teacher and principal evaluations become more closely tied to student achievement scores, more and more class time is being devoted to test preparation. In some classrooms, even as professional development initiatives push teachers to promote more student discussion, engagement, and discovery-based learning, the pressure of the state tests results in less of each actually being done, while at the same time increasing the number of worksheets and practice tests.

In this top-down system, the meta-framework for teacher accountability (and funding) flows from the Feds to states, local school superintendents, principals, department chairs, and finally, at the end of the line, to classroom teachers.

Is it any wonder that teachers, along with their students, feel positioned at the very bottom of the educational food chain?

While many talented educators are packing it in and leaving the profession, there are many who are committed to their calling and who stay. Dedicated to becoming more effective teachers, they work diligently to help their students succeed on achievement tests, but they also strive to connect with them in meaningful ways and even to make a difference in their lives outside the classroom. They struggle to maintain the profession as a path with heart, and thus they seek mastery.

So, where can they—and you—turn for help?

If we're going to fulfill our calling to a larger purpose, if we're to succeed at "changing heads, changing hearts, changing history," and "bringing harvest home," then we're called to consider embarking on a lifelong learning journey. The calling asks that we walk a road less travelled—a path of self-reflection, self-awareness, and practice. For it's our inner life, reflected in our personal attributes and our classroom presence, that will ultimately motivate and inspire our students to succeed academically and to fulfill their own larger purpose and life-calling.

Whether you're an elementary school teacher surrounded by bright student-artwork, and this morning you passed a line of smiling, wriggling, lovely first graders who greeted you with a dozen chirpy "Good mornings!" (and perhaps a hug or two)...or you teach at a middle school or high school where the sounds of the school band practicing echoes in the halls and mixes with the smells of food being prepared in the cafeteria...or you hear the laughter of students discussing a scene in *Hamlet* and at the bell you see the crush of students cramming the halls and filling them with joyful noise and unrestrained energy...

...no matter where your school building is located, and no matter its physical condition, it's good to remember you are *blessed*, for you are in no ordinary workplace.

"Teachers Wanted: Must Love Students"

To the Editor:

We travel around the country helping urban and rural high schools increase college enrollment rates for economically disadvantaged students. The principals and administrators we meet say that what they need are teachers who love students.

Yes, they admit, a teacher needs the most sophisticated tools and curriculum, as well as expertise in psychology, neuroscience, pedagogy, learning differences, and academic standards. But it is the teacher who has the greatest capacity to care and to connect with the students who makes the biggest difference.

One Buffalo school principal said, "The school district cannot mandate what matters, and what matters most is the ability to love the students."

Where do we find such teachers, and how can schools of education deliberately begin to cultivate their students' souls?

— Keith W. Frome, Buffalo, New York (*The writer is the National Director of Education for College Summit, a nonprofit group.*)

CHAPTER 2

THE POWER OF RELATIONSHIPS

Only those leaders who understand the dynamics of trust in schools will be successful in fostering vibrant school communities well-equipped to meet challenging new demands. Trust impacts schools at their bottom line: student achievement.
— Megan Tschannen-Moran

Making Connections

It was my junior year of high school, and Mrs. Keehan called me to her desk after English class.

"Peter," she said, smiling, "I've noticed that you love to read."

"Yes, Mrs. Keehan," I replied.

"I want to give you something; but before I do, you have to promise me you'll keep it a secret."

Her voice was soft and intimate, quite different than the voice she used during class. "Yes, I promise." She opened the drawer of her desk, removed a paperback book, and handed it to me. "I picked this book especially for you. I think you'll really enjoy it."

I looked at the title: *The Lord of the Rings.*

"Remember your promise, Peter."

"Yes...and thank you!" I mumbled as I turned and left.

I had never heard of J. R. R. Tolkien, and the first chance I got I began reading the paperback. I was soon mesmerized, and I fell in love with the book. It was as if Mrs. Keehan knew me and knew what I'd like. I felt special. I worked harder for her than any other teacher that year. There was no way that I wanted to let her down. *After all, we shared a secret: a special relationship.*

Forty years later, at my high school reunion, as a group of old friends and I sat around a table reminiscing, I broke the promise I had made to Mrs. Keehan and told the story of the secret book. My friends looked shocked. One after another, each of them who had taken her class told their own story of being called up after class, sworn to secrecy, and given a book chosen especially for them. Mrs. Keehan had built a special bond with each of us. I don't think the different books she hand-picked to give us were what made us feel special. No, it was the intimate, heartfelt tone in her voice, the shared secret, the feeling I had of being special.

I don't remember much about my junior year. Most of my teachers' names and what they taught me has faded; but Mrs. Keehan, and the *special* relationship, the connection I had with her, is with me still, as it surely is with every student she taught that year—and possibly throughout her career.

Relationships Are Key to Academic Achievement

Mrs. Keehan's "secret" connection with her students reminds us that much of what inspires children to learn happens in the personal space (the "heart space") between us and our students. Relationships are at the very heart of successful teaching; and it's our hearts that prepare the soil and provide the nutrients for trusting relationships to grow.

While positive relationships carry many important social and emotional benefits, the reality of today's educational environment is that teachers are being held accountable for their students' academic progress, as measured on achievement tests. It might be nice to talk about the "heart" and about "trust," but today our professional survival as teachers depends on our students' succeeding on both state and national exams. If they don't achieve academically, our jobs are in jeopardy and we may be looking for a new career.

The good news is that relationships and trust are two, almost magical keys to increasing student achievement. There are a myriad of research studies that confirm and quantify their importance. Here is just a sampling:

Positive trust relationships between students and teachers:

1. Are much stronger predictors of gains in math in elementary and middle school than class size, teacher experience, or the availability of instructional supplies (Sara Rimm-Kaufman, 2002).[1]

2. Are even more significant for "at risk" students (Baker, 2006).[2]

3. Are better predictors of improved reading performance for children exhibiting aggression, hyperactivity, anxiety, depression, and learning problems than for children without these risk factors (Baker, 2006).[3]

4. Help kindergarten children continue to develop better academic and social skills as they near their middle school years, in contrast to those that experience conflict in their teacher relationships in kindergarten (Berry and O'Connor, 2009).[4]

5. Produce more engagement and motivation in their students. (Battistich, Schaps, and Wilson, 2004).[5]

6. Are a critical factor in predicting which schools will make the greatest gains in student achievement and which will sustain

those gains over time. In schools where there is greater levels of trust, student achievement is generally higher and the gains are lasting (Bryk and Schnieder 2002).[6]

7. Are a critical vehicle not only for improving student success but also for overcoming some of the disadvantages of poverty. For teachers to help students access the opportunities that schooling can provide, they need to build trust (Watson, 2003).[7]

8. Contribute to students' developing better psychological well-being, more rewarding relationships with parents and others, academic success, higher school completion, better employment experiences, and fewer problems with peers (Bryant and Zimmerman, 2003; Bubois and Silverthorn, 2005; Greenberger, Chen, and Beam, 1998; McDonald, et al., 2007; Rhodes, Ebert, and Fischer, 1992; Zimmerman, Bingenheimer, and Notaro, 2002).[8]

9. When combined with strategies that empower students, and validate them as individuals, the relationships contribute to their academic success and their personal growth and produce more engagement and motivation (Birch and Ladd, 1997).[9]

10. Contribute to developing students who are less likely to avoid school and are more self-directed, more cooperative, and more fully engaged in learning (Birch and Ladd, 1997; Klem and Connell, 2004).[10]

The academic, social, and personal benefits of trusting classroom relationships are truly breathtaking!

So why is it that most people in the educational establishment view building trust and classroom relationships as an informal pursuit—something to do if teachers have the time and not a primary strategy we employ for improving our students' academic success? Is it because relationships and trust are viewed as personal, soft, and maybe even "squishy"?

What are we to do with the overwhelming evidence that it's crucial to our students' academic success and personal growth that we develop personal relationships with them and work on opening our hearts? Do we continue to double down on drill and practice, worksheets, seat time, pull-out and push-in interventions, extended school days, extended school years, and (fill in the blank_____)? Or do we expand the conversation with our principals and superintendents to include the importance of establishing trusting relationships in the process of learning?

It's no secret that students work harder for teachers they care about. Reaching out purposefully, and opening our hearts to building relationships with our students, is a warm invitation to them to join you in the grand learning process. When your students implicitly trust you, and feel trusted in return, they're more likely to be positively engaged in learning.

> The youngster who really made me understand [the power of relationships] was Eddie. I asked him one day why he thought he was doing so much better than last year. He gave meaning to my whole new orientation. 'It's because I like myself now when I'm with you,' he said. —Teacher quoted by Everett Shostrom in *Man, the Manipulator* [11]

Trying to teach without developing relationships can be very slow going. We may make progress, we may cover material, check the boxes, and get things done, but it all takes a lot more effort without good relationships with our students. When strong, trusting relationships are in place between us, the teaching and the learning take less energy and are much more enjoyable and rewarding than everybody just slogging through classes filled with mistrust, indifference, and passive-aggressive behavior.

Making Time for Relationship Building

Yet even when we acknowledge the important benefits that building trusting relationships can bring, it can seem overwhelming to actually set aside enough time to build them. After all, the day is short, we're already busy, and there is so much to teach.

> "I don't have time for this! I have 125 students. I can't be a psychologist, a social worker, and a teacher!" —Teacher

Building relationships and trusting classroom environments doesn't have to take a great deal of time. Whatever time it does take is a wise investment.

> I was the tallest boy in middle school. I felt awkward and self-conscious, and slouched to fit in. One day as I walked down the hall Mrs. Edwards remarked that she thought I looked handsome in the shirt I was wearing. It made me feel great. I made it a point to walk in that part of the hallway the next day and, sure enough, she had a big smile and another compliment ready for me. After that, I never missed a chance to walk past her, and she never failed to compliment me on how nice I looked. By the end of the year I wasn't slouching anymore, I was standing tall. I never had her as a teacher; but she made a huge difference in my life. —A student

> Too often we underestimate the power of a touch, a smile, a kind word, a listening ear, an honest compliment, or the smallest act of caring, all of which have the potential to turn a life around. —Leo Buscaglia[12]

Research, as well as our own experience, teach us that building relationships and creating trust are not supplemental activities. They must be conscientiously cultivated and sustained; and to do this well, we're challenged to cultivate our gifts, our personal attributes, and our hearts. For it's this inner "self" that engenders and elicits trust. Trust is the seed from which all relationships grow.

> "I understand what you're going through" builds trust.
> "I'm listening to you" builds trust. "We're in this together"
> builds trust.

When trust is present, relationships are strong and amazing things are possible.

REFLECTIONS

1. Trusting relationships with our students are essential for improving academic achievement. When trust is lacking, teaching and learning are impeded.

2. Strong teacher–student relationships in the early grades have a lasting, positive effect on academic and social skills through middle school.

3. Making time to build relationships is important to our students' academic success and personal growth.

ACTIONS

1. Assess trust levels in your class. On a scale of 1–10, with 10 being the highest, how would you rate the level of trust you have in your students? How do you think they would rate the level of trust they have in you? What objective criteria can you point to to support your assessment?

2. Do you consciously take steps to build trust? If the answer is "yes," what are they and how could they be improved? If it is "no," what steps could you take to build more trust?

Start Close In

Start close in,
don't take the second step
or the third,
start with the first
thing
close in,
the step
you don't want to take.

Start with
the ground
you know,
the pale ground
beneath your feet,
your own
way of starting
the conversation.
Start with your own
question,
give up on other
people's questions,
don't let them
smother something
simple.

To find
another's voice
follow

your own voice,
wait until
that voice
becomes a
private ear
listening
to another.

Start right now
take a small step
you can call your own
don't follow
someone else's
heroics, be humble
and focused,
start close in,
don't mistake
that other
for your own.

Start close in,
don't take
the second step
or the third,
start with the first
thing
close in,
the step
you don't want to take.

— DAVID WHYTE

CHAPTER 3

CULTIVATING THE "SELF"

The teacher as a person is more important than the teacher as a technician. What he is has more effect than anything he does.
— Jack Canfield

The Power of "Self"

The idea that our students' academic success is dependent on both our professional skill and our personal attributes may be difficult to accept. Equally difficult is the idea that fulfilling our potential as educators asks that we explore the preeminent role that we, as human beings with our unique life experiences and values, play in both the academic and personal success of our students.

But in some ways we already know this. We sense that it's not how smart we are, the pedagogy we choose, or how much we know about our subject area that determines our classroom success. Year in and year out we've seen well-intentioned teachers enter the profession with great expertise in their subject areas, yet fail miserably in the classroom. Something doesn't click with their students. Great teachers possess something intangible.

Calderhead (1996), Pianta (1999), and Watson (2003) have described teaching as an intensely psychological process and believe a teacher's ability to maintain productive classroom environments, motivate students, and make decisions depends on her personal qualities and the ability to create personal relationships with her students.[1]

Ray McNulty, from the International Center for Educational Leadership, writes:

> If there is not a high level of positive relationships, students will not respond to higher expectations. We must not underestimate the sheer power of relationships in making our schools more effective. Relationships do not become a new standard or replace rigor and relevance. They are a way to improve learning.[2]

"Soft" Heart or "Courageous" Heart?

It's easy to deny the wisdom of our heart, the importance of our personal attributes, and the power of trust in learning—because they seem abstract. They deal with areas of our lives that are generally considered strictly personal. Even the language we use to discuss them diminishes the importance of the "self" by referring to them as "soft" skills, implying their lack of importance when, in fact, as we've seen in the research, they're absolutely essential skills.

Some classroom practitioners declare they want practical, concrete solutions to the challenges they face, not talk of ethereal things they associate with the heart. They believe that bringing the personal side of ourselves into the classroom dilutes learning. For them, "opening the heart" means showering students with false praise and encouragement. It means inflating their grades so that students don't feel bad, and taking the focus off learning and putting it on self-esteem. They interpret teaching with heart, and building trusting relationships, as a call to become friends with students, rather than fulfilling their role as effective teachers. They think that teaching with heart means eroding standards and indulging in "feel-good" education.

Teaching with heart doesn't mean that anything goes or that we need to indulge our students by compromising our own standards. Nor does it mean that academic performance is overlooked or that we allow ourselves to be manipulated or pushed around. Instead, we're teachers made up of strong hearts, heroic hearts, hearts that persevere. We let nothing get in the way of what's best for our students because we possess committed "hearts of service" and, like athletes who play with heart, we give teaching our all.

> Kate, a young teacher in the South Bronx, struggles with the question of whether to do a unit on *Romeo and Juliet* with her class. They are mostly Hispanic, low-income students. Will the language be too difficult? Will it be viewed as weird and uncool? Can she present it in a way that will engage and motivate them? Failure will be painful for her both academically and in terms of classroom management; for she knows her students won't sit quietly if they're bored or uninterested.
>
> Kate loves the play and during her student teaching watched her own Master Teacher successfully guide her students through it. Trusting her heart, she decides to take the risk. She works hard and spends many late nights developing activities, lessons, and materials to bring the play to life for her students.
>
> Several weeks later, a shy sixth grader from a broken home, who lives below the poverty line, grips his side and staggers around the classroom, as he plays the death scene in *Romeo and Juliet*. Kate, like many in the class, is leaning forward,

captivated by his performance. He may be hamming it up; but he's giving it his all. The class has come to love the play. Later that day, he and several other students get a special hall pass and come to Kate's classroom. They want to direct other students on how to play the scene. Kate's courageous heart becomes a heart filled with the joy of teaching.

Good teachers teach the mind, but great teachers also ignite the heart.

Still, a chorus of serious educators insist that we choose between teaching the minds of our students, the way we've always taught, or that we indulge ourselves by appealing to their hearts—but this is a false choice. It's not a one or the other, "either-or," proposition. There are mountains of good research that indicate we can do both; in fact, we *need* to do both.

It may be difficult to wrap our heads around it, but our challenge is to embrace the seeming paradox that the human heart contains the keys to unlocking the gifts of the mind. Those of us who haven't fully awakened to our own inner lives may achieve some degree of success in the classroom, yet much will be missed, for it's difficult to light the fire of curiosity, creativity, and learning in others if our own heart is closed.

The good news is that the classroom presence and personal attributes of a great Master Teacher can be learned.

A New Professionalism

Cultivating the "self" is not to be confused with the growing "touchy-feely," self-esteem training industry. Its seminars may make us feel good, on a personal level, though they rarely translate into sustained improvements in our classroom. If self-improvement were as easy as taking notes at a seminar, every teacher would be a master. We know intuitively that cultivating the personal attributes of a Master Teacher simply cannot happen as a result of a one-day program. Rather, it's a journey—a challenging one, not to be taken lightly nor without ample preparation.

Ironically, the idea of deliberately cultivating our hearts, personal attributes, and classroom presence is widely considered off limits to most professional development and teacher preparation initiatives. Why? Because being a "professional," for most of us, has always meant keeping our personal and work lives separate.

If we have a spat with our spouse or partner before heading to school in the morning, we do our best to check our anger at the classroom door, because we don't want it to affect our teaching. We already know that no matter what goes on outside the classroom, we must be professional when we enter it. So we do our best to separate our personal self from our professional self, and therefore we look at personal development as strictly a private matter, confined to the self-help shelf at our local bookstore.

> There is a classic story of a drunken man searching for his lost keys under a bright streetlight. A passing policeman stops to help him.
>
> After searching around for some time, he asks the man, "Are you sure you lost your keys here?"
>
> "Oh, no," the man responds. "I lost them on the other side of the street!"
>
> "Then why are you looking for them over here?" the perplexed police officer asks.
>
> The drunk replies, "Because the light's better over here."

Like the inebriate, many of us tend to look for our answers, especially to our professional challenges, in the places with the best light. We look outside ourselves ("Top 10 Tips for a Perfect Classroom") for what we think are professional solutions. Few of us venture into the less travelled, dimly lit places of the heart—the places where the answers may actually lie.

So how do we deal with the fact that our values, our beliefs, and our inner life, reflected in our classroom presence, personal attributes, and soft skills, are fundamental to our professional success? Do we continue searching for answers under the nearest streetlight, or do we search in the right places?

Perhaps our definition of professionalism needs an upgrade. Maybe the wall that separates the personal and the professional needs to be replaced with a more permeable, translucent membrane.

Leaving the well-lit streetlight to search for answers within ourselves requires courage and trust; for cultivating the self is a journey into sacred terrain. It's a road less travelled, and navigating such sensitive territory requires a serious commitment. The journey must be embraced carefully and voluntarily, but what better place to explore ourselves than the melting pot of the classroom, where our beliefs and values are challenged daily and where we're called to keep our mind and heart open to the needs of our students ?

A Lifetime Journey

There is no single way to teach that is appropriate for every teacher, nor one that will be successful with every student. Discovering what works for you and your students is an evolving journey that great teachers travel over their lifetimes. It's a journey of self-discovery and an invitation to walk a path well worn by dedicated teachers before you.

And, as with most of life's great journeys, there are few maps (or streetlights) provided. Along the way, we'll find the voice of our inner teacher. We'll explore our self and our gifts more carefully, and what we discover may be surprising. Of course, we'll make our share of mistakes, and if we're lucky we'll find the lesson in each one, then gently forgive ourselves for our missteps, because cultivating compassion for others begins with compassion for ourselves.

Are you open to explore the path to mastery and to my proposition that, no matter your subject matter, grade level, or years of experience, *you teach and learn from the inside out*?

The rewards of the journey? The true fruits of the profession: guiding our students to academic success, as well as helping them grow personally, emotionally, and socially. Of course, our students need to navigate the educational system as it is, flaws and all; but we also want them to be excited about learning and to explore the many horizons that lie before them and within them.

Cultivating the Master Teacher within us will enable us to build confidence in those students who seem tentative, help us to coax any downcast eyes upward, and help us to develop our students' shy whispers into powerful voices.

If our commitment to our students and our self remains true, we may find that, over time, we become much better educators with a deepened appreciation for the joys of teaching. We'll discover the wisdom of the heart—the inner voice that reinforces what we already know: that teaching isn't about filling empty vessels but about lighting the fire of curiosity and igniting a universe of passion in the hearts and minds of our students.

So it is that, to fulfill your calling and purpose, you're asked to continue the hard work of learning; for *becoming a Master Teacher is really about becoming a Master Learner*. It's *you* who must take the first tentative steps on the new and unfamiliar path that leads to mastery.

It should come as no surprise, then, that teaching and learning is about *you*...

...because all change, all effectiveness, emanates from *you*.

REFLECTIONS

1. Our personal attributes are key to our classroom effectiveness as well as to our students' academic and personal success.

2. Schools with the highest levels of trust, built on positive relationships, have the highest levels of student achievement.

3. The classroom presence and personal attributes of a great Master Teacher *can* be learned.

4. For teachers who aspire to mastery, *professional* development and *personal* development are synonymous.

5. Teaching Mastery requires a lifelong commitment to learning *and* to practice.

ACTIONS

1. Create an inventory of your personal attributes (strengths and weaknesses). How would you describe the best and most effective attributes of your personality? The least effective?

2. How would your students characterize your personality? Your teaching style? What attributes would they say they admire? What attributes would they say they dislike?

3. What personal practice or practices do you engage in to improve your teaching? Describe them and tell how often you engage in them. What results have you seen?

Losers

They sat around me, sprawled on crudely carved, graffiti-filled desks with small metal and wood chairs. It was nearing the last day or so of the school year, and this particular group of boys didn't want to leave. It was the last period of the day, and I sat on a desk with my feet on a chair in front of me.

"Mr. Reilly, it's not your fault," said Billy, the leader of the group. It was sort of strange that these particular boys were hanging out in my classroom, for they had been the students who had gotten the least out of my class, and school in general. They were common visitors to the principal's office and denizens of detention.

Billy continued, "We're losers. No way you were going to teach us." He smiled at me. The others smiled, too.

"You tried, though." Now they became a little more serious. "You're not so bad for a teacher." The others nodded agreement.

"Guys, you aren't losers. You're good kids," I responded.

"Nah; we're definitely losers. We hate school. It's boring. You tried to make it fun; but we didn't need half the stuff you tried to teach us."

Kevin chimed in, "Some of the books we read were cool."

Michael added, "I liked the goofy music you played, and the poetry."

I shook my head and remarked, "You guys are smart. Why did you make it so hard on yourselves?"

It struck me how kind they were being. How appreciative. They accepted the consequences of their actions, and they were peaceful with their plight. They weren't angry or holding grudges, because they felt they had been treated fairly. It was as if they were professionals at this, as if they were saying, "No hard feelings...business is business. You, Mr. Reilly, were just being you—'teacher'—and we were being us—'losers.'"

But they *weren't* losers. They were really nice kids with good senses of humor. They were just completely out of place in school. They had other, more important things going on in their lives. If you saw them outside of school, you'd be amazed at their competence and confidence.

On one occasion outside of school, Billy piped up: "Lemme look under the hood, Mr. Reilly." A moment later, "I think I see the problem. I'll fix it." Sure enough, Billy reached into the bowels of the complex machine that was my car and began to work.

These were the rejects, the freaks. They were like a Greek chorus in my teaching life because they were so real. They weren't going to "play" school like the others. They weren't going to "pretend" this was important to them. I could count on them reflecting back to me the best and worst of my teaching. If I was at my best, I would see them engaged fully. Anything less, anything that was not relevant, not well planned, not taught well, and they would find something else to keep them busy. Generally, that would be something that got them in trouble.

They're all grown men now. I suspect that some must have children of their own. They're frozen in time for me, in my life's memory. So many students entered and left my life; but these, the losers, remain. They represent the best of those I taught. Too young to really be my friends; but always my soulmates.

CHAPTER 4

WAKING UP

Once the soul awakens, the search begins
and you can never go back.
— John O'Donohue

Awareness

Self-awareness is like finding the "You Are Here" arrow on a map. It helps orient us before setting out on our journey. But finding that starting point isn't as easy as it sounds. Most of our behaviors have been part of us for so long that they've become automatic, habitual, and, to some extent, invisible. (Though not to others...especially our students!) Much of what's happening around us, and within us, happens under the radar, unnoticed.

John is a veteran science teacher who wants to foster more student discussion in his classroom. He's stifling student dialogue because he talks too much; but he's so enthusiastic about his subject he can't seem to control himself. John's totally unaware of his tendency to crowd out his students with his own talk and gets frustrated with them because, no matter what he does, they don't engage in the discussion. Of course, then nothing changes.

When our habits and behavior patterns remain unconscious and automatic, we're powerless, so we simply continue doing what we do, thoughtlessly unaware. In a sense, we're captives to the patterns of the past. But when we wake up and become aware of what we're doing, we're in a much better position to engage in new, more-effective behaviors. Unfortunately, when we're in the grip of a habit (an automatic pattern of behavior), like John is, we compulsively repeat it even when it's not effective.

Because John is unaware of how his monologues are contributing to the lack of free-flowing discussion, he blames his students. He hasn't yet awakened to his own accountability. Like John, the first step for most of us on the road to mastery is to engage in a healthy dose of self-reflection —the kind that leads to self-awareness.

To get the results he seeks, John will have to shift his focus from others (his students) to himself.

Awareness Follows Attention

We know from experience that it's difficult for students to learn when they're distracted and unfocused. So, it should come as no surprise that one of the most important prerequisites for exploring and learning about our self is to practice focusing and managing our own attention. Learning to turn our attention inward creates the conditions for our awareness to come forward.

Our awareness is a quiet voice that we rarely hear because it's drowned out by the endless chatter of our minds. The wisdom of our hearts needs stillness, for our awareness is like a shy woodlands creature. It runs from us if we crash through the brush calling for it. But if we stop and sit quietly and patiently in the midst of the silent forest, it steps out from the brush and approaches us cautiously.

When we put our full and undivided attention on something, like our "sit bones," for example, it doesn't take long for us to begin to feel the awareness of that area growing. Suddenly, things we had missed before, like the softness of the seat cushion, a feeling of general warmth in our posterior, and a slight tingling of the skin, all begin to come into our field of awareness.

Wherever we put our full and focused attention, awareness follows. So it is that if we are to walk the path of the Master Teacher, we, like John, will have to focus our attention on our inner self.

Managing Our Attention

Richard Strozzi Heckler, in his book *The Anatomy of Change*, says,

Without the ability to manage our attention, it manages us.[1]

Our attention can be a wild thing, and difficult to control. Our minds are constantly thinking about one thing or another, and wandering, undisciplined, from thought to thought virtually every second of every day.

This is a great time to turn to the *Practices* section and try the "Sit Bones" activity. This activity allows you to experience, firsthand, how deeper awareness follows our focused attention.

We may be driving to work and suddenly our mind drifts to planning a lesson, reliving an incident from the previous day, or simply indulging in a pleasant daydream. The car is traveling at 50 mph and we're on autopilot. We aren't paying attention to the road and before we realize it we're surprised to be pulling into the parking lot of our school, and we think,

"How the heck did *that* happen?"

When we let our minds wander aimlessly this way, we aren't fully aware of what's happening within us or around us. We can miss a great deal—maybe even something as important as another inattentive, unaware commuter in an SUV, perhaps running a stop light. Whether we're driving or teaching children, being inattentive, unaware, and unfocused—not being fully "present"—can be quite dangerous.

When we *do* focus our attention, a surge of awareness follows. Suddenly the landscape is no longer a blur. We see the sunrise over the distant hill, the children laughing while texting at the bus stop, the wave of a neighbor wishing us "Good Morning"—*and* the speeding SUV running the stop light.

Inner Focus

One teacher described the process of becoming self-aware, this way:

> If we notice how we feel, pause, and take a breath, it gives us the time and ability to reappraise the situation.[2]

This simple statement provides us with a wonderful road map for exploring the self.

Notice, feel, pause, take a breath, and then reappraise.

Like a row of dominoes falling, each action triggers the next; but the first domino, the "noticing," sets everything in motion. If we don't notice how we feel or can't sense what's going on within us, then we won't pause, breathe, or reappraise the situation, so we'll simply forge ahead blindly. Self-inquiry asks that we pay attention to everything, but especially to what's happening within us.

> I was giving a lecture to a group of teachers in my graduate course and noticed that they seemed particularly bored. I did a quick self-check and noticed that my breath was high and in my chest, and I was barely breathing as I spoke. My overall sense of energy was weak. I realized that I was teaching solely from my head and not including my heart. I took a deep, settling breath, and dropped my energy from my chest to my legs, which had the effect of bringing me back from my heady thoughts that clearly weren't connecting with my class. Immediately, my voice took on a different, warmer, quality; my energy became more grounded; and my

presence more open. The students may not have been consciously aware of it, but the mood and energy of the room had changed. —Adjunct professor

Awakening

Alas, the world has no cookie-cutter molds for developing great teachers, nor one way to teach that works for all. So undertaking an exploration of the self is, by definition, a first-person, subjective process. There are no right answers—only the wisdom that we discover through self-reflection, self-knowing, and self-awareness. If we combine deliberate self-reflection with a commitment to practice, we may find that we can develop a stronger sense of purpose, presence, and connectedness, each being a part of the "infrastructure" of the Master Teacher.

> John, the talkative science teacher, began meditating and self-reflecting in the evenings after school. He decided that rather than blaming his students for their lack of class participation and trying to coax them into engaging in discussions, or ruminating about why they seemed so passive, he would simply and directly ask them why they weren't doing so.
>
> He was surprised when they responded that he "talked too much" and that he wasn't really giving them a chance to speak. It first shocked him, then resonated with him, for it wasn't the only time John had been told he talked too much. Deep down, he knew that what his students were saying was true. His lifelong habit of filling in uncomfortable silences with his own voice was now clearly in his conscious awareness.
>
> Now that he was aware of his habit, and conscious that it was hindering him from reaching his goal of lively class discussions, he was in a prime position to change his behavior.

He decided that whenever he posed a question to the class he would silently focus on his breath, the way he did when meditating before going to bed. Focusing on his breath calmed him down and helped him tolerate the occasional uncomfortable silence, while still allowing his students space and time to gather their thoughts, summon the courage to speak, and then comment.

To his credit, John also recruited his students to be "feedback partners." He asked his class to let him know whenever they noticed him falling back into his old habit of "talking too much." Needless to say, he and his students shared a few laughs whenever they brought an occasional slipup to his attention.

Over time, John's classroom was transformed. Class discussions were lively, they were passionate, they flowed authentically...with John carrying less of the burden and with students much more participative and content.

Learning from and through the Body

Awakening our self-awareness means exploring the "feeling" self as well as the thinking self. We engage the "feeling" self by paying attention to the sensations, emotions, moods, and life of our body. We look within and we allow ourselves to feel. In this sense, our body, our mind, and our heart become our textbook, our inner teacher. It's an inside-out approach to learning.

The idea that we can learn *from* and *through* our bodies is not the common sense. In Western learning the mind and body are treated as two separate and distinct entities with the body perceived as subordinate to the mind, simply there to carry our brain from classroom to classroom. Approaching learning this way starves us of an important part of our natural heritage, the organic wisdom within us.

> It [focusing on the holistic self] allows us to come home to
> the body and to re-experience the harmonious integration
> of sensation, feeling, mind, and spirit that is ours by nature.
>
> —Hartley [3]

As we travel the path to mastery we'll learn new ways to "come home to the body" and create safe and quiet spaces for our inner teacher to emerge. Because it's a gentle voice, it's sometimes difficult to hear, but it will be instrumental in guiding us through the many twists and turns of our journey.

Awakening to Our Mood

Just as our minds are filled with endless streams of thought, our bodies are filled with sensations, rhythms of excitement, and moods that are constantly working within us. These bodily sensations have a profound influence on our behaviors.

For instance, when John asked his students a question and encountered only silence his heart would begin to beat faster, his breath get shallower, and his face start to flush. The feeling inside him was one of anxiety, and vulnerability. He found it difficult to tolerate these sensations, so he tended to dissociate from them and skip over the silence by filling it in with his own words ("after all, I'm the teacher," he told himself). Becoming aware of the bodily sensations that were influencing him and cultivating ways to tolerate them was an important part of John's eventual classroom success.

A basic practice for becoming more deeply self-aware is to do the "sit bones" practice, and after a few moments shift our attention from our posterior to our breath and then let our awareness feel its way into our mood. It may take a few moments to sense it, but what we find is sometimes surprising. Our mood might be one of ambition, gratefulness, curiosity, wonder, frustration, anger, sadness, resignation, anticipation, fearfulness, and so on.

Since our mood influences everything we do, it's especially important to see how it's affecting our teaching. For example, if we're in a mood of frustration and anger, we may not be in the best state for connecting and building trusting relationships with our students. A mood can lodge in us for a few minutes, a day, several months, sometimes even years. Once we become aware of our mood, we're able to take steps to change it if necessary; yet it all starts with inner awareness. After all, we can't do what we want until we know what it is we're actually doing.

It takes patience, faith, and courage to look within. Patience because our attention is easily distracted and there's no way to force our inner wisdom to surface. Faith because we're not used to trusting our own voice when it *does* appear. And courage because what we notice when we look within isn't always pretty. We may discover a mood or a few personal behaviors, attitudes, or beliefs that aren't reflections of our best self (like John's talkativeness), and realize that they may be drags on our classroom effectiveness.

Developing an inward focus is the beginning of self-awareness—*the foundation of self-knowledge, self-fulfillment, and self-cultivation.*

Seeing with New Eyes

As we travel the path to mastery and become more self-aware, we begin to notice changes in our perceptions. It's as if we've put on a pair of reading glasses and the blurred writing on the page before us suddenly comes into focus. We can read the words clearly for the first time. It's the "opening of eyes long closed."[4]

In a thought-provoking interview on PBS, the physician-turned-life-guru Deepak Chopra put forth the idea of thinking of our life as a mirror:

Your life is a reflection of you.

His statement seems innocuous enough, though there's more to it than meets the eye. What he's saying is that if our life (or our classroom) is productive, safe, and joyful, *or* if it features lots of drama, conflict, frustration, and anger, then most likely it's a reflection not of others but of *us*.

Wow! That hits a nerve.

Sure, we know that some students will enter our classrooms with issues, both academic and emotional, and there's no doubt there are many systemic educational issues such as a lack of resources or large class sizes that are entirely outside our control. Nevertheless, how we choose to deal with them is our choice. We can be in a mood that is critical, angry, negative, and discouraged—which creates conflict and closes doors. Or we can choose to deal with these issues with an open heart, understanding, self-confidence, and resilience—each of which *opens* doors.

Reflect on the types of in-school conversations you've been having lately. Do they have a negative tone? Is there a mood of frustration? Are you easily drawn into nonproductive bull sessions with colleagues in the lunch room or on a walk around campus? Ask yourself: are these conversations a reflection of your best self?

Teaching isn't easy; no news there. From time to time we'll undoubtedly lose our focus and get lost in a negative mood or unproductive byway as we journey. Often we can find our way back to the path by focusing our attention on the mirror that Deepak Chopra talked about—the mirror that is our life. For it's in this mirror that we'll find the clues, the inner wisdom, and the self-awareness we seek.

As we begin to see new distinctions in old landmarks in the familiar territory of our lives (and in our classrooms), we may realize that what we thought was rock-solid fact may not be as solid as we once believed. The towering mesa of our self-regard that we see may be an illusion. It's not unlike pulling back the curtain in a darkened room for the first time and seeing a brilliant summer day dancing outside our window.

"OMG!" we cry. "I've been missing all of this?!" And "What *else* haven't I seen?"

However we experience our awakening and our growing self-aware-ness, it can be glorious and uncomfortable at the same time. Glorious because we have a vague sense that it's high time we rise from our slum-ber; and uncomfortable because when we do rise, we lose most of the major landmarks we've been using to navigate through our lives to this point. It's as if we've been relying on routes shown on an old map to get us where we want to go, and then realize the map is far out of date; it can't help us anymore. We need to blaze and travel a new path. So what do we do now?

Discoveries like these can be quite startling. Like the point in the 1939 film *The Wizard of Oz* when Dorothy opens the door to her Kansas farmhouse, which has been dropped into a strange land, the film suddenly shifts from black and white to color. We realize, "I'm not in Kansas anymore!"

As we awaken on our journey toward achieving Master Teaching skills, we sense that for each new door we open there is an old and familiar one that is closing. We may want to turn around and head back to familiar territory, but really, there's no going back—at least not by the way we came. We can't be "unaware" once we're aware. We can't "un-see" once we've seen.

Our shell is cracked and light is seeping in. We're already beginning to grow.

Our journey is well under way.

REFLECTIONS

1. The exploration of "self" is by definition a first-person, subjective process. There are no "right" answers.

2. Wherever we focus our attention, awareness follows.

3. We can learn from and through the body by noticing our bodily sensations, feelings, and energy, holistically, rather than simply thinking about things with our minds. The body, mind, and spirit are one entity.

4. An important template for cultivating the "self" is to "notice, feel, pause, take a breath, and reappraise before acting."

5. Our mood can affect how we see the world and how we interact with our students.

ACTIONS

1. Try the "sit bones" activity (*Practices* section) a few more times. Each time, focus your attention on a different part of your body (feet, hands, nostrils, and so on). When you finish the activity, record the bodily sensations, feelings, and energy you felt.

2. Identify your mood. Is it a mood that is helpful and effective, or one that is not? Start a practice of checking in on your mood before beginning each of your classes.

3. What is the mood of your class? Your students?

The Way It Is

There is a thread you follow. It goes among
things that change. But it doesn't change.
People wonder what you are pursuing.
You have to explain about the thread.
But it is hard for others to see.
While you hold it, you can't get lost.
Tragedies happen; people get hurt
or die; and you suffer and get old.
Nothing you do can stop time's unfolding.
You don't ever let go of the thread.

—WILLIAM STAFFORD

CHAPTER 5

RECONNECTING TO PURPOSE

If you don't know where you're going,
any road will take you there.
—Lewis Carroll

Reconnecting to Purpose

Before we get too far along on the journey, it's important to declare our destination and *why* we're traveling to it. Our *why* is the "for sake of what?," meaning our purpose for cultivating the self and for pursuing mastery. It's our ground, our inner compass—it's who we are. It isn't an intellectual construction of the mind, nor is it a mission statement written by a committee (one that sounds good yet is soon forgotten). Our purpose is a deep, *felt sense* of personal meaning. It's a calling to something larger than ourselves.

Like John, the physics teacher in chapter 1 who realized he was no longer the teacher he wanted to be, we may realize that thinking deeply about our purpose isn't something we do very often. It's no wonder, as we noted earlier, since the daily challenges of teaching can be all-consuming and since there's never enough time to do everything we want to do. Like the stonecutters in the earlier classic story, it's easy to find ourselves doing our jobs with our eyes cast down and our nose to the grindstone rather than fixed on the stars (our students!).

When we take the time to connect to our purpose, we deliberately lift our gaze to the far horizon of possibility. We experience the spaciousness of the world, its magnificent beauty, and the freedom it offers. When we choose to look up, to look out and look within, we recognize anew the incredible universe we're blessed to be part of, as well as the tremendous opportunity we've been given. It becomes crystal clear that we're building cathedrals, not simply chipping stones.

While we may be a small part of this big world, the road to Teaching Mastery asks that we center our "self" around life's big questions:

> "For the sake of *what* have I been given the privilege of this life...and the opportunity of being a 'teacher'?" —Teacher

The answer to our question might be colossal and brimming with idealism:

> "I want to truly change the world we live in." —Teacher

It can also be more personal:

> "I'm a teacher because I want to make a positive impact on students. I have a genuine love of learning and want to pass that on to students. When students see a teacher who loves the material and wants to learn more, they become intrigued, as well." —Teacher

No matter what your answer, as long as it comes from your heart, and contributes to others, it holds great power.

> "Our motive, if we are to be truly happy, must be an external motive—it must be service. It must be giving, not getting." —Richard Leider[1]

It's from this place of giving, our "aligned center," that we're most powerful and most effective, both in and out of the classroom. Our life's purpose and calling is the foundation of our journey toward Teaching Mastery. Grounding ourself in it gives us the courage to set off on an unfamiliar and deeply personal pilgrimage. It helps us persevere when we feel discouraged, so that when we're called to take a difficult stand for our students, or for ourselves, we'll do so in the knowledge that we're reflecting our deepest values and core beliefs.

Have you ever been lucky enough to see a hawk tracing delicate circles in a clear blue sky? It looks so effortless. It can soar for miles with the slightest adjustment of its wings. How does the hawk do it? How can it reach such great heights so easily?

If you're disconnected from your purpose, or if you're not clear about it, there are ways to reconnect with it. I've included several activities in the *Practices* section to help guide you.

The hawk finds, and then rides, a warm updraft of air: a thermal. Our life's purpose is very much like a warm thermal. When we find it, it can propel us high and far. It supercharges our soul.

Vocation and Avocation

As we deepen our connection with our calling and purpose, we also deepen the connection between our self (personal attributes, and heart) and our teaching. Of course, we'll have to fight the traditional mindset that claims that "work is work" and that anything personal is not appropriate in our professional life. Yet aren't we most fulfilled when our life's purpose and our work are aligned?

Robert Frost says it brilliantly in the last stanza of his poem "Two Tramps in Mudtime"[2]:

> My object in living is to unite
> My avocation and my vocation

As my two eyes make one in sight.
Only where love and need are one,
And the work is play for mortal stakes,
Is the deed ever really done
For Heaven and the future's sakes.

This may not be the common view, though the workplace may in fact be the very best place for us to engage our true self, because the connection between our personal attributes, our heart, and our ability to create trusting relationships is directly related to the effectiveness of our work with students. The link between who we are as people and who we are as teachers is impossible to sever.

> "It is very hard to separate the person and the teacher. The values, morals, and methodologies one has as a person and as a teacher intertwine so intricately that it's difficult to find the exact point where one ends and the other begins. The concept of caring is also intricately woven throughout the personal and professional being I am as a teacher. A person who cares in life is a person who cares in their profession as well. Therefore, my personal and professional goals as a teacher are inseparable." —Teacher

We know by now that there's no way to completely compartmentalize our personal self from our work self. It's an artificial barrier, which over time inevitably breaks down. After all, we can't help being who we are. Our personal attributes, beliefs, and attitudes eventually seep into our teaching. We have only one self. There is only one you.

As Robert Frost in effect reminds us, *we are most effective and most fulfilled when we are fully human, fully ourselves...even at work.*

REFLECTIONS

1. It's easy for us to lose sight of our "calling" and larger purpose amid the day-to-day requirements of our job.

2. We perform at our best when we have a deep connection to purpose and meaning, especially when our professional and personal "callings" are one.

3. Maintaining a mission-driven sense of purpose sustains us when we encounter obstacles and challenges.

4. It's impossible to completely compartmentalize our personal "self" from our professional "self."

ACTIONS

1. What is your larger purpose and calling? Write your purpose as a simple declaration. Use the format provided in the Practices section.

2. Each morning for a week, before your first class, your first meeting, or your first cup of coffee, sit quietly for a moment. Feel your purpose again. Write it on a piece of paper. Now, list at least one intention for the day that flows from that purpose, no matter how small; for example, "I will recognize the gifts of just one of my students."

A Teacher's Story

Late in an extraordinary afternoon of professional development, the staff engaged in an activity meant to consolidate the wonderful work they had done during the day. They were asked to take a few moments to reflect on some event in their professional lives that had made a significant impact on them.

They were to spend a few minutes reflecting on their careers and then form small groups of four or five to share their stories. A number of individuals cast their eyes down, shutting out their surroundings. A few looked out the room's large windows, seeming to be peering back into the depths of days long past. Some began writing notes immediately. What they wrote were the memories and stories that represented the touchstones of their work lives.

When enough time had passed, they began to draw their chairs into comfortable circles and to share their stories aloud. There was passion, there was respect, and, here and there, a few laughs, a few tears.

When it was time to debrief the small groups, the staff became silent and shy, much like their own students. A hand went up from a group in the front.

"I don't want to tell my own story, but she has a story that really touched us," a man said as he stood up, gesturing to a veteran teacher in their group. "If she's okay with it, I'd like to tell her story." The shy woman nodded her assent. The storyteller remained standing as he began.

"Mrs. Alvarez was in her second year of teaching in a bad part of the Bronx. She was a second grade teacher, and she had a quiet boy named Carlos who was struggling to learn to read in her class. Carlos was living with his mother in a run-down apartment building in the neighborhood. His father, who had left the family a few years before, lived in the same building, but whenever he saw Carlos, he would ignore him. He acted as if he didn't know him. He wouldn't talk to him or even nod 'hello.' Needless to say, this devastated Carlos, and the impact of it seemed to drive him deeper into his shell. He had no confidence, and his struggles at school only added to his misery. Mrs. Alvarez worked as hard as she could to help Carlos to read, but things weren't going very well.

"Toward the end of the year, Mrs. Alvarez received her assignment for the coming year. She was given the opportunity to move to a position in another school. It was a good school and she was really excited.

"One day after school, Carlos's mother came to see Mrs. Alvarez. She spoke in broken English, saying, 'You have helped my son Carlos this year. He talks about you at home. Thank you.'

"Mrs. Alvarez nodded modestly.

"Carlos' mother began again, saying, 'He still cannot read. I worry for him. If you would teach him again, I'm sure he would learn. I think he will disappear if he has to start again with a new teacher. I beg you, Mrs. Alvarez, please stay with my son. Teach him to read.'

"Mrs. Alvarez went home that night and thought about Carlos's desperate mother. It was the plea of an immigrant mother who loved her son and knew that so much of his life hinged on his ability to read. Carlos was definitely the kind of quiet kid who could easily slip through the cracks in a crowded class and fall further behind.

"After several days, Mrs. Alvarez made her decision. She called the principal of the new school and politely turned down the offer to transfer to her 'dream job.' Instead, Mrs. Alvarez asked her own principal to let her move up a grade with Carlos's entire class. He agreed.

"The next year went by quickly. Mrs. Alvarez taught as best she could, always giving Carlos a bit of extra attention. She hoped that things would click for this shy, frightened little boy. Carlos's mother didn't come back to the school that year.

"Many years later, Mrs. Alvarez was teaching at a school in another neighborhood in the Bronx. It was the end of the year and she stayed late to pack her things and clean out her class-room. When she was done, she left the building to walk across the street to her car. As she got to the corner, she stumbled and dropped a sheaf of papers on the concrete sidewalk. A gust of wind scattered the papers in all directions. She sighed and without hesitation stooped to pick them up.

"At that moment, two tall boys rounded the corner and saw her predicament. They both began chasing down and retrieving the papers that by now were all over the intersection. She smiled gratefully as the taller of the two boys approached her with a handful of papers and a smile. 'Thank you, young man,' she said. 'Thank you very much.'

"Suddenly the young man's smile disappeared. He mur-

mured, 'Mrs. Alvarez?'

"In an instant they both recognized each other. It was Carlos, grown now, straight and tall and handsome. Without hesitation or self-consciousness, they embraced.

"'Carlos, you're so big. You're a man now!' Carlos beamed with happiness.

"The second boy, who had been busily chasing papers, interrupted to ask incredulously, 'Excuse me, you...you're Mrs. Alvarez?'

"She looked at him, 'Yes, I am, and do I know you?'

"Carlos's friend was very serious. 'No,' he said, 'you don't know me, Mrs. Alvarez; but I know you. Last week, Carlos and I graduated from high school. Carlos was the valedictorian of the class. He gave the commencement speech in front of the whole school. He told us about a teacher named Mrs. Alvarez that helped him learn to read, and cared for him, and inspired him. It was this teacher, Mrs. Alvarez, to whom he owed his success. Are you *that* Mrs. Alvarez?'

"She stood there looking at the two young men. She began crying very sweet tears of joy. Carlos embraced her again. Carlos's friend insisted on shaking her hand."

The teacher telling Mrs. Alvarez's story paused for a long moment. He was tearing up, but he managed to say, "That's the story she told us in our group.... I had to share it."

The room was completely silent. Our hearts were swelling. Here and there teachers were wiping their eyes. Applause burst spontaneously from the entire staff.

CHAPTER 6

Putting Ideas into Action

Live your beliefs and you can turn the world around.
—Henry David Thoreau

Embodying Our Beliefs

A wonderful story is told of a mother in India who takes her son to visit Mahatma Gandhi.

> "Great One! My son eats too many sweets," the mother says. "He is putting on weight, and his teeth are in peril. Will you please tell him to stop eating so much sugar!"
>
> Gandhi looks at the boy and the mother and says, "Bring the boy back in two weeks."
>
> The mother leaves, a bit disappointed and confused, but returns with the boy two weeks later.
>
> Gandhi looks at the boy and says calmly, "Please stop eating sugar. It is not good for you."
>
> The mother smiles, but before leaving turns to Gandhi and asks, "Great One! Why didn't you say this two weeks ago?"
>
> Gandhi smiles back and replies, "Two weeks ago *I* was still eating sugar."

Mahatma Gandhi embodied his beliefs. He didn't separate his words and his actions, as so many of us do. Because he had such high levels of integrity he was deeply trusted by millions. It's this kind of trust that we teachers hope to develop with our students. The challenge is that believing (and saying) one thing and doing another is so common in our culture that we take it for granted. But when what we think and what we say are out of synch with how we act, we're perceived by others, including our students, as unreliable, even untrustworthy. We don't show up as having a high level of integrity. To create the kind of trusting relationships we want with our students, we, like Gandhi, need to "walk our own talk."

> We are now at a historical transition in which it is crucial that learning be placed in the context of action, as a way of being in the world, instead of being simply intellectually smart.
> —Richard Strozzi-Heckler, *The Leadership Dojo*[1]

We *Know* What to Do

A multitude of research describes the attributes of our most effective teachers. One study, Laura J. Colker's "12 Characteristics of Effective Early Childhood Teachers," lists the following as among the more important attributes of early childhood teachers: passion, perseverance, willingness to take risks, pragmatism, patience, flexibility, respect, creativity, authenticity, love of learning, high energy, and sense of humor.[2]

Letitia Usher, in her research study titled "Nurturing Five Dispositions of Effective Teachers," lays out her own list of characteristics, which include empathy, positive view of others, positive view of self, and authenticity, as well as meaningful purpose and vision.[3]

You're probably not surprised by such research. Educators have an innate understanding that great teaching is composed of a variety of professional skills and personal attributes. When asked, we have no problem generating exhaustive lists of the attributes of Master Teachers. So, whether it comes from research or from daily classroom experience, it's pretty clear that most of us in education know the characteristics—what I call the *personal infrastructure*—of a Master Teacher.

Yet if we know so much about the makeup of Master Teachers, why are they so rare? Think back to your own teachers. How many would you classify as great? Why is there such a disconnect between what we know is effective classroom behavior and what actually goes on in our classrooms? Why aren't we "walking our own talk"?

Knowing versus Doing

Intuitively, most of us understand that knowing what it takes to be a great teacher doesn't always translate into being one.

> Mr. Ellis, a high school principal, calls his faculty together for a meeting after school. He begins his presentation using PowerPoint slides. The slides are chock full of text, and he turns his back to the group and reads directly from the screen. The faculty members are being polite but are bored. They think, "We can read the slides ourselves. Why not just give us the presentation handouts and let us go home?"
>
> Suddenly, Mr. Ellis turns to the group and says with a laugh, "I know it drives people crazy when presenters read from their PPT slides. I hate that, too."
>
> Everyone laughs with him and is relieved that he's become aware of what he is doing, but within minutes, to his faculty's dismay, he's back reading his slides again.

Mr. Ellis is a smart man. He has a good sense of effective protocols for presentations. He's even self-aware enough to point out what he's doing wrong to his staff. He's a great example of someone who knows what to do but doesn't yet embody his intellectual knowledge. Instead, he falls back on the familiar, comfortable, and quite boring behavior of reading his slides verbatim. He doesn't yet "walk his talk."

The journey to mastery asks that we take what we "*know*" about effective teaching and put it into action, to embody it. John, the talkative science teacher, worked to embody one new behavior for his class—let's call it patience with silence. He wanted the behavior integrated into his body so he could call it forth as needed. This was much more than simply knowing (intellectually) that it would be good to be patient when silence arose during class discussions.

Remember, the purpose of our journey to mastery isn't to obtain insights about ourselves but rather to cultivate our best and most effective self and then to bring it to our teaching. Learning, in this context, is a commitment to taking new action. It would be good here to entertain a new definition of learning, one that distinguishes between "knowing" and "doing."

> In my country we say that knowledge is only a rumor until it is in the muscle. —Old proverb in New Guinea

Is it possible to take what we know about the personal attributes of Master Teachers and embody that knowledge? Or is it a matter of having been lucky enough to be born with the right characteristics, talents, and inner qualities? This is a question that comes up a great deal in the teaching profession.

Moving from Ideas to Action

K. Anders Ericsson, a researcher at Florida State University, has found that it's not what you're born with but instead how consistently and deliberately you practice to improve your performance that makes the difference between average and master-level performance in any endeavor.

> We agree that expert performance is qualitatively different from normal performance...[but] *we argue that the differ-*

ences between expert performers and normal adults reflect a
life-long period of deliberate effort to improve performance in
a specific domain. —"The Role of Deliberate Practice in the
Acquisition of Expert Performance"[4]

This is far from surprising. After all, we wouldn't expect to learn to play basketball by reading about it, discussing it, or watching others play it. Athletes practice and musicians rehearse so that they have embedded in their bodies the very skills they need to excel.

Teaching is no different. Old behaviors that we've practiced for years generally don't change overnight. It's precisely because our personal attributes and classroom presence are so deeply rooted in the core of who we are (our self) that they are difficult to change, and yet so powerful when they are.

Traditional professional development programs—listening to lectures, reading books, writing about and discussing effective teaching with others—can be most helpful. Yet it's rare that these approaches result in sustainable new behaviors. If we want to embody what we know about great teaching, it helps to acknowledge that we can't simply think, read, or talk our way through the process. Maybe the old joke says it best:

> Two tourists in New York City become lost on their way to a recital. They see a man walking by with a violin case. They stop him and ask:
>
> "Do you know how to get to Carnegie Hall?"
>
> The violinist answers without hesitation, "Practice, practice, practice."

So there it is—the secret formula, "practice." It's the unvarnished, and profoundly simple, way to embody new behaviors and achieve Teaching Mastery.

REFLECTIONS

1. Research has identified many of the important personal attributes of successful teachers. We have a good idea of what constitutes the personal infrastructure of a Master Teacher.

2. Still, knowing what to do and being able to do it—how to embody it— are two different things.

3. We can learn to embody the attributes of a Master Teacher by engaging in deliberate, sustained practices.

ACTIONS

1. Initiate a daily practice of starting the day by restating the purpose that you've written.

2. Identify a colleague in your school who you feel is an exemplar educator. Identify one of this person's characteristics that you admire most. When you do this, generally (and unconsciously) you are projecting a characteristic that you also have within you. Is it a characteristic you'd like to develop further? What practice could you begin to cultivate that characteristic?

Laird and Bob

Two high school students, Laird and Bob, poked their heads through my doorway late one afternoon. Laird, a truly unique kid, was one of the brightest boys in the school. His dad was a reporter for the local newspaper, and the son had inherited his father's curiosity and persistence. He marched to the rhythm of his own drummer. I guess back in the day he'd be called a nerd.

"We were down in the principal's office and we saw two boxes stacked there," Laird told me, excitedly. "They're computers!"

This was the dawn of the age of personal computers (the early 1980s), and there was not a single computer in the school district. No labs, no classroom computers, no office computers. This was a time when blue duplicating fluid, filmstrips, and opaque projectors were at the top of the technology food chain in schools. As I found out many years later, Apple had shipped two of its new computers to high schools throughout the country as a marketing ploy, including two to our school.

Laird continued, "Mr. Ellis said we could set them up and use them if we had a member of the faculty to supervise us. How about it, Mr. Reilly? Would you supervise us?"

I agreed, and the next afternoon Laird and Bob, his best friend, were setting up these strange machines in the back of my classroom. I hovered behind them as they slipped the large 5¼"computer disks into the disk drives and turned the first computer on. I remember the drives making a loud grinding noise and I thought the boys might be breaking them, but I kept my mouth shut and let them proceed. Suddenly, on the monitor, a green word appeared.

[HELLO]

It was magic!

Each day, they showed up and worked with the two computers. I sat at my desk correcting papers, but really I was more interested in what they were doing. There wasn't much "supervising" to do, since the two boys seemed to be the only ones in the school interested in the new machines. They talked as they typed, read manuals, and poked around the innards of the devices.

But they caught my attention one day when they produced a short riff of electronic music. "Listen to this, Mr. Reilly. Isn't it cool?"

I was curious. "How did you guys *do* that?"

It was the beginning of a wonderful relationship. I started sitting with the boys and they didn't withdraw but instead treated me the way I might treat a well-intentioned though academically overmatched student. They talked and acted in a shorthand that was clear to them but, well, Greek to me. Still, they always took time to explain what was going on, and eventually I began to see some potential in the computers. They introduced me to word processing, taught me some Basic programming, and invited me to play computer games they had copied from some unknown source. The three of us explored and played—and learned together—for the remainder of the year.

Throughout the more than 30 years since Laird, Bob, and I shared our first computer experiences, I have told audiences the story of the two boys who changed my life. One day in the late 1990s I wrote a blog post to express my appreciation for the two, for had they not sought me out, had they not been so generous with their time, had they treated me like a teacher rather than a fellow learner, my life would have been drastically different.

Several months after I published the blog post, Laird, who must have Googled his name, posted this comment:

> It is amazing what you find when you search for your own name. Mr. Reilly, I may be 42 now, but it still just seems strange to call you "Pete." I am really humbled to know that I had this effect on your career path, especially since your willingness to supervise the work we did with computers that year set the course for mine.
>
> I remember staying after school to work on the computers every night that year until the janitor kicked us out to lock up, and I also remember getting the occasional phone call from you at home. I have related the story many times in my career, but in my version it was always you who changed the course of my life.... The love of computers which you instilled in me that year always stuck with me, so much so that I am now the Senior Desktop Architect for [a major bank] based in Austin, TX.
>
> I will be getting in touch with you soon to catch up.
>
> —Regards, Laird

CHAPTER 7

THE PRACTICE OF "CENTER"

At the center of your being
you have the answer;
you know who you are
and you know what you want.
—Lao Tzu

The Merriam-Webster dictionary describes *center* as "a source from which something originates."

What Is Center?

Center is a "felt" state, therefore something difficult to describe in words. It's both a state of mind and a physical phenomenon—a blending of body, mind, and spirit. When we're centered, we feel physical balance and harmony in our posture, breathing, and center of gravity, which enables us to act in harmony with our values, beliefs, and purpose. To be centered is to live in the immediate and ever-changing balance of these systems.

When we teachers are in this state of holistic alignment, our classroom presence is most powerful and effective. When we're in the state of being centered we're aware of what's going on within us, open to what is happening around us, and connected to the things we care about most.

The challenge is that sometimes our fears, moods, and anxieties knock us off center. We can get distracted by our thoughts (living in our heads), lose contact with our hearts, and dissociate from the uncomfortable sensations that may be coursing through our bodies (as they do with John, the overtalkative physics teacher). The problem is that when we're thinking about the past, or anticipating the future, we aren't fully present in the moment. Our attention and therefore our awareness are elsewhere. This is true both in and out of the classroom.

In the classroom, when we're off-center not only do we miss teachable moments and opportunities to build strong relationships with our students, but we also tend to fall into the compulsive grip of past habits and automatic behaviors. Why? Because when we encounter stressful situations that make us feel anxious, we revert to familiar behaviors (well-practiced ones) that make us feel safe and comfortable. We do this unconsciously, and whether or not they're appropriate or effective.

There's a Hawaiian proverb that aptly describes "center" without the typical jargon:

He po'i na kai uli, kai ko'o, 'a'ohe hina puko'a.
"Though the sea be deep and rough,
the coral rock remains standing."

When our soma (body, mind, spirit) is balanced, we're like the coral rock firmly anchored beneath the sea; no matter how rough the ocean's surface, the excitement, emotions, moods, fears, and anxieties of a difficult situation aren't likely to sweep us away from our home. True, we're fully aware of the chaos that may be swirling around us, but we're not driven by it. The energy of the situation doesn't lead us to engage in unhelpful, even destructive, automatic responses and historic patterns. Instead, we're centered.

Finding Center

This all sounds good, but how do we find center? Try thinking back to a point in your life, maybe before you were about to take part in some big, stress-inducing event, when someone noticed your nervousness and admonished you to "Relax!," "Calm down!," "Take a deep breath!," "Just be yourself!"

That was great advice. Research shows that stressful situations produce muscle tension, increased heart rate, elevated blood pressure, excess stomach acid, and more. But while our heart is beating fast, our body pumping adrenaline, and our mind racing, it's not easy to feel calm or relaxed. We know that calming ourselves would be a good idea, yet it doesn't seem possible. The situation is simply too charged with excitement. The problem is that no one ever taught us the mechanics of how to calm ourselves. We just don't know how to do it.

While the prescription offered earlier…

Notice, feel, pause, take a breath, and reappraise before acting.

…is spot on, it's easier said than done. Why? Because when we're triggered by a stressful situation, we react impulsively. Our ability to self-regulate is compromised. We're filled with powerful bodily sensations, and thoughts stream through our minds at lightning speed.

> Transitions cause my mind to race in a million different directions. This [centering] gives me a chance to just be, to clear the chalkboard in my mind. —Teacher in CARE

Clearing the "chalkboard" (or Smartboard) and creating the space "to just be" are both important parts of the journey to Teaching Mastery. Whether we're dealing with the daily work and routine of the classroom, or with a particularly challenging and stressful situation, centering ourselves in the moment gives us a place of calm and clarity from which to act effectively. It's the foundation from which we'll build the classroom presence and effective behaviors of a Master Teacher.

So, how can we learn to be more present, more open, more centered?

Learning to Center Through Meditation

Centering ourselves in the present moment is actually quite a simple process, though one that is challenging both to execute and to sustain. In its basic form, centering is an extension of the "Sit Bones" activity (chapter 4), but instead of focusing on our backside we'll focus our attention on the breath entering and leaving our body. When we focus like this, the roiling waters of our mind begin to calm, and as they do, our anxieties and fears begin to fade into the background. At the same time, our bodily functions (heart rate, blood pressure, nervous system, and the like) begin to return to normal. Calming our mind centers our body.

Focusing on the breath this way is a common meditation practice and is often referred to as "mindfulness." Mindfulness is a widespread practice in the Buddhist world, but for our purposes we'll approach it from a strictly secular point of view. It's simply a powerful practice that helps us focus our attention, develop our self-awareness, and become more centered.

This would be a great time to try the mindfulness meditation practice contained in the *Practices* section.

A number of organizations work with educators to help integrate mindfulness into their teaching practice. One of them, CARE (Cultivating Awareness and Resilience in Education)[1]—an educational research program that utilizes mindfulness to promote awareness, presence, compassion, reflection, and inspiration in educators—reports that mindfulness practice reduces work stress and helps teachers respond, rather than react, to challenging student behavior. That, in turn, improves the overall classroom climate and helps students succeed academically, socially, and emotionally.

It [mindfulness practice] has given me the tools and skills to be more calm and centered. In a particular situation, I can act in response to what is needed in the moment, rather than reacting to it.... This creates an atmosphere of confidence, trust, and more joy in the classroom. —Teacher in CARE

Observing the "Wild Mind"

For beginners, engaging in mindfulness meditation can be extremely frustrating. Initially, we may not feel especially calm or aware, either during or after our practice. The more we try to focus on our breath, experienced meditators soon learn, the more active our mind becomes. We can't seem to get it to calm down. No matter how hard we try to concentrate, it simply goes where it wants to go, and we get swept away with it.

One breath, two, three...and then our mind drifts to an incident that happened earlier in the day, or last week. Seconds or even minutes go by before we even realize that we aren't paying attention to our breath. Suddenly, our self-critic appears and chides us for not doing the practice right. We think, "I'll never get it. There's something wrong with me!" Our inner critic continues berating us, and we notice that, instead of concentrating on our breath, we're paying attention to our own, internally produced, negative chatter. Now that we're aware that we've been distracting ourselves, we note it, and we come back to the present and to our breath again. Our entire practice goes like this, one breath at a time, over and over.

There's no reason to get discouraged simply because our mind is so wild and easily distracted.[2] The good news is that losing our focus and bringing it back, gently and nonjudgmentally, is a vital part of mindfulness practice. By gently and nonjudgmentally managing our attention and awareness, we're breaking old patterns of thought and building a foundation of self-regulation and self-awareness.

> Neuroscientists have found that everyone has a default state.... [T]his state thinks about the future and the past, makes judgments, and categorizes and compares everything.... Mindfulness practices like yoga and meditation can temporarily take us out of the default state and into an experiencing state. —Kelly McGonigal, "Brain Power"[3]

The simple principle behind mindfulness is that if we keep taking our awareness back to the breath—over and over again—then our mind gradually quiets down and we become more centered, more able to recognize and observe our thought patterns. With practice, when thoughts arise, we notice them in a detached manner without being triggered into engaging with them. We simply notice the distracting thought and let it go. Once we learn to become an impartial spectator, we're better able to recognize old, habitual patterns that no longer serve us, and then we can reshape those patterns in new directions.

> Mindfulness-based interventions...may be ideally suited to help reduce teachers' tendency to make automatic, reactive appraisals of student behaviors that contribute to emotional exhaustion and support a mental set associated with effective classroom management. —John Meiklejohn, "Integrating Mindfulness Training into K-12 Education: Fostering the Resilience of Teachers and Students"[4]

Physical Centering

As noted earlier, there is also a physical aspect to finding our center. When our body is centered and we put our full attention on it and feel it, we find that doing so calms and centers our mind, too. Our body, mind, and spirit, after all, are a single entity and can't be separated.

Here is a body-centering practice you can do anytime during the day:

Physically, change your posture. When standing, lower your center of gravity and evenly distribute your weight between both legs, balancing left to right and back to front. Feel both your feet as firmly grounded and balanced between the ball of the foot and the heel, with your knees slightly bent. Let your shoulders relax and hang on your skeletal frame naturally. Relax your jaw and soften your eyes. As you do this, focus on your breathing. Notice that your mind is slowing down and you're becoming calmer and more focused on the present moment.

We can practice centering and mindfulness while sitting or while walking, doing the dishes, vacuuming the house...or teaching. When our body is balanced and relaxed, our breathing calm, and our attention focused, we're grounded, fully present in the moment, and able to move quickly and appropriately when necessary. This is our "center." This is the foundation of the Master Teacher.

Tending the Garden

Centering and mindfulness are the generic tools, the rake and hoe, that help prepare the soil of our innermost self before we plant a new garden—and they are the tools that we'll use to tend it once it begins to grow. They are so important that it's recommended that we practice them every day for 10 to 20 minutes.

Each time we engage in mindfulness and bring ourselves to a state of center, we till and soften the hard-packed soil (meaning the hard-wired neurological pathways) of our past habits and compulsive behaviors. When we bring our attention to the present moment and focus our awareness, nonjudgmentally, on what that moment has to offer, we nourish the garden and make room for the elements of our best self, the inner self of the Master Teacher, to grow. It's here, in the stillness of our quiet mind, that we're most likely to find the soft voice and wisdom of our inner teacher.

> Human nature is not a machine to be built after a model, and set to do exactly the work prescribed for it, but a tree, which requires to grow and develop itself on all sides, according to the tendency of the inward forces which make it a living thing. — John Stuart Mill

Be mindful, though, that "center" is not a pedagogical technique. It's neither how we teach nor what we teach, but instead it's the inner foundation from which we teach...

...and from which we grow.

REFLECTIONS

1. Center is a state of being where our body, mind, and spirit are grounded and calm. When centered, we are fully present and open, free of anxiety and fear.

2. Being centered is key to effective teaching.

3. When we don't manage our attention, it manages us.

4. Mindfulness practice trains our attention by focusing on our body (through the breath). Part of the practice is to gently refocus on our breath, without criticizing ourselves when we become aware that our mind is wandering.

5. Regular mindfulness practice reduces stress and allows elements of our best "self" to emerge.

ACTIONS

1. Begin or end each day with 10–20 minutes of mindfulness practice.

2. Before engaging in your practice, state your purpose and intention silently.

3. Throughout the day (especially before beginning a class), engage in a one-minute centering/mindfulness practice by stating your purpose and intention to yourself, taking a few deep conscious breaths, and turning your attention inward to feel the sensations of some part of your body (your feet resting on the floor, your hands quietly in your lap, your face muscles relaxed, your head balanced calmly on your spine).

The Benefits of Mindfulness and Centering

The positive benefits of mindfulness and centering are universal. When you engage in "centering and mindfulness," you do the following:

1. Manage your attention, focus, and energy, allowing you to build your awareness of self.

2. Live deliberately in the present moment, opening yourself to experience your classroom and your students more fully.

3. Exercise your will by returning to the object of your attention (breath, body) when you become distracted, thus building your self-confidence and power.

4. Observe yourself without self-judgment, thereby building self-acceptance and, with it, compassion for yourself and others.

5. Experience the world holistically, through your body, as well as through your thoughts.

6. Train yourself to stay calm in challenging situations and to interrupt your own historical behavioral patterns that might not be appropriate.

7. Let go of anxiety and fear so that you're able to experience a calm center.

CHAPTER 8

RETURNING TO CENTER

Not being able to govern events, I govern myself.
—Michel de Montaigne

Amygdala Hijack

Sitting alone in a quiet place and doing mindfulness and centering practices is quite different from trying to remain centered in a classroom full of hyperactive teenagers or a wriggling, squirming mass of enthusiastic elementary school students. Maintaining center while in action is challenging because there are so many ways to be knocked off-center, and without a doubt our students, their parents, or our colleagues will find ways to do it.

"Center" is like the content of a lesson plan. No matter how much time we spend preparing, it's when we bring our plan to the classroom that life happens. After all, we're teaching students from various backgrounds, with different personalities and experiences, and each of them responds to us differently. An activity that worked well with one class can flop with another. Students who at one moment seem engaged and interested can be sent into chaotic excitement by a flash of lightning and a peal of thunder, or even a few snowflakes falling from the sky, or someone giggling in the back row.

Being centered is similar. It's our foundation, yet the unexpected is bound to happen, and when it does it can throw us off. It can "trigger" us.

When we're triggered, an ancient "fight, flight, freeze, or appease" (FFFA) response fills our body with adrenaline and other complex hormones. It's a reflex mechanism that helped our primitive ancestors survive in emergency situations. When we're in the FFFA state, our bodies operate reflexively at their highest levels of alertness. We're able to run a little faster, jump a little higher, and perhaps, if needed, like our ancient ancestors, throw a spear a little further. FFFA is not a choice but a reflex.

> Marty is a ninth grader with an attitude. He takes advantage of every opportunity to make Mr. Jones, his teacher, look the fool; and Mr. Jones unwittingly plays his part. One day he asks Marty to throw away the candy he's eating in class. Marty rolls his eyes for all to see, walks defiantly to the front of the room, and throws the candy into the metal garbage can with purpose. It clangs loudly as he smiles triumphantly at the class.
>
> Mr. Jones snaps and begins berating him angrily, and Marty begins to talk back disrespectfully. Mr. Jones grabs his arm and hauls him out of the classroom and into the quiet hallway. He leans close to him and in hushed but angry tones whispers a torrent of threats, laced with profanity.

When Mr. Jones completely loses it with Marty, his own FFFA kicks in (what we call an "amygdala hijack").[1] His body is flooded with hormones meant to help him survive an attack from some prehistoric predator like a wooly mammoth, even though the actual situation with Marty the child is far less threatening. Mr. Jones's reaction ends up being way out of proportion for the incident. At the same time, his ability to make rational decisions breaks down. Instead of taking the most appropriate action for the situation, Mr. Jones defaults to survival behaviors stored for millennia in the deepest part of his brain. The problem is that Marty is not a saber-toothed tiger that needs to be slain. He's a ninth grade student.

It's inevitable that we're going to be confronted with behaviors and events that have the potential to trigger us. Our students know (intuitively) which buttons to push to knock us off center. The question is, can we stay calm and relaxed? Can we maintain our sense of center?

Getting Back Faster

The answer is, NO! We're definitely going to get triggered and thrown off center. We're human beings, not zombies. We have feelings; we have reflexes.

> My students think I never lose my center. This is not so;
> I simply notice it sooner and get back faster.
> —Morihei Ueshiba, founder of Aikido[2]

Like Morihei Ueshiba, it's inevitable that we're going to be triggered. Our task is to recognize when we're not centered, and bring ourselves back.

It helps to familiarize ourselves with the bodily sensations we feel when we're knocked off center and locate the sensations we feel within our body when we're triggered. For example, we might be holding our breath, sensing a heaviness in our chest, perhaps feeling a churning sensation in our stomach, or experiencing a tightness in our jaw or neck. What we feel and where we feel it will be unique to each of us.

I feel a knot in my stomach, my legs feel restless, and my

heart pounds louder than usual. The one thing that causes me the most trouble is my voice. It takes on an edge, and I have the tendency to sound harsher than I'd like to. If I know the feelings that signal this response, I can stop for a moment, take a breath, and calm down. —Teacher[3]

Notice how this teacher who has spent time building her self-awareness and a foundation of center gets triggered but, because she's familiar with the sensations associated with it, she becomes aware, stops, breathes, and returns to center where she is calmer. Like her, once we become familiar with our own triggering sensations and learn the centered feeling, we can recenter ourselves before our amygdala gets completely hijacked.

He who controls others may be powerful, but he who has mastered himself is mightier still. —Lao Tzu

Getting back to center can be as simple as using a "One-Breath Meditation," where we take a single, deep, conscious breath that breaks the flow of events, calms us for a moment, and brings us back into balance. Taking one *conscious* breath can create a tiny pause that provides us with a split second of calm. It creates a toehold that can help us take control of our attention—and also, in some small way, of our actions. The more we break the stranglehold of our thoughts and the flood of emotions and bodily sensations that sweeps over us, even if only for an instant, the quicker we're able to recover our center.

Wow! I was amazed this week. Instead of raising my voice, I tried taking a deep breath to calm myself down. I can't believe how well this worked. The kids actually began calming down, too. —Teacher in CARE

As we learn to regulate our responses to triggering events in the classroom, we begin to build a reservoir of trust with our students. The more centered we are, the more they open to us and to what we have to teach. It's really that simple.

John, the veteran physics teacher in chapter 4, who tended to engage in long monologues and generally talked too much, reflected on one additional practice he used to keep his attention focused:

> Because my tendency in class was to talk too much, I began doing a brief meditation before class to connect with my intention to limit my speaking, and to remind myself to listen more. Because I start class having prepared myself to speak less, and listen more...I'm much more aware and notice quickly when I begin to get the old talkative feeling. Once I notice what's happening I stop the train before it gets rolling. The results are surprising and the more I practice, the easier it's getting.

If we're ever to break our personal cycle of reflexive, reactive, and automatic behaviors, it will greatly help if we become familiar with the bodily sensations, emotions, and moods that arise when we're triggered. Then we can practice the conscious pause, the deliberate cleansing breath, and the return to a calm center.

We may never be able to avoid the daily incidents that trigger us in our busy personal and professional lives, but by learning to quickly return to center we can greatly diminish their power.

REFLECTIONS

1. When we're "triggered" by an unexpected emotional, psychological, or physical event, it causes an automatic FFFA response. None of these reflexive reactions are "wrong," for they're ancient survival mechanisms.

2. When we're triggered, we aren't centered, so our capacity for rational and appropriate responses breaks down.

3. Because we are human beings, we can't avoid being "triggered," but we can learn to return to center more quickly.

4. We can practice different methods of recovering our center until we find the most effective ones.

ACTIONS

1. Identify your typical FFFA response. Do you move away from the stimulus (flight)? Move toward the stimulus (fight)? Become immobilized (freeze)? Or try to "make nice" with others (appease)?

2. Identify some thing, person, or behavior that "triggers" you. Make a list of the classroom triggers that you've experienced.

3. What bodily sensations do you feel when you're triggered? Where in your body do you feel them? What can you do to return to center?

Autobiography in Five Short Chapters

Chapter One

I walk down the street.

> There is a huge hole in the sidewalk.

> I fall in.

> I am lost.... I am helpless.

> > It isn't my fault...

It takes forever to find a way out.

Chapter Two

I walk down the same street.

> There is a deep hole in the sidewalk.

> I pretend I don't see it.

> I fall in again.

I can't believe I am in this same place.

> But, it isn't my fault.

It still takes a long time to get out.

Chapter Three

I walk down the same street.

>There is a deep hole in the sidewalk.

>I see it is there.

>I still fall in...it's a habit...but,

>>my eyes are open.

>>I know where I am.

It is my fault.

I get out immediately.

Chapter Four

I walk down the same street.

>There is a deep hole in the sidewalk.

>I walk around it.

Chapter Five

I walk down another street.

—Portia Nelson

CHAPTER 9

Personal Tendencies and Beliefs

Let go of your old tired habits and
plant new habits in fertile soil.
—Harley King

Automatic Responses, Habits, and Personal Tendencies

Centering and mindfulness are powerful practices that train our attention, increase our awareness, and move us from a mind-driven, thinking experience to a more holistic, heart-centered one. They bring calm and clarity, and they create the conditions for meaningful personal change.

But while centering creates the environment for change, much like tilling the soil and fertilizing a garden before planting, it doesn't guarantee a successful crop. Over time, our deepening self-awareness and the voice of our inner teacher leads us to a place where we begin to notice how our own lifelong patterns of behavior may be stunting and crowding out parts of ourselves that want to emerge and bear fruit.

Examples of Personal Tendencies Getting in the Way

Each of us has personal tendencies and habits that, over a lifetime, have shaped our personalities and who we are. Most of them are useful and effective, but generally there are a few that aren't. Personal tendencies, habits, and historical patterns of behavior manifest themselves in different ways, both in and outside of the classroom, yet they're almost always automatic and often invisible to us.

Mary, Francine, and Brian

Mary is a teacher who tends to shut down her feelings. She is bright and enthusiastic, but because she doesn't show her enthusiasm outwardly, she has difficulty connecting with her students. Her voice is mostly a monotone, showing little emotion. Her students perceive her as someone who doesn't care and lacks passion. She seems aloof.

Francine has a pessimistic streak and tends to foresee the worst outcomes in most situations. She brings her pessimistic attitude to the classroom and avoids any activities that are creative or risky. "After all," she thinks, "they probably won't work anyway."

Brian has always tried to fit in to new situations by being a "worker bee" and sacrificing his own needs for the needs of others. In the classroom, his tendency leads him to get over-involved with his students and his work. He takes care of everyone but himself and in the process feels taken for granted, angry, and resentful.

Mary, Francine, and Brian each have lifelong personal tendencies that influence their classroom presence, their effectiveness, and how their students perceive them. Their tendencies have become deeply interwoven into the fabric of who they are. In each of the examples above we might say that the teacher's personal tendencies are stunting or limiting their performance.

The Origins of Our Tendencies and Beliefs

Our personal tendencies are generally manifestations of our beliefs about ourselves and the world around us. We've held many of these beliefs our entire lives. But where do they come from?

Most often when we are young we adopt them both consciously and unconsciously, from our family, our friends, and our community. We absorb them from institutions like religion and school, as well as the social culture around us. Who we are—the "self" we are—is in large part the sum of the beliefs we've internalized over our lifetimes.

> Two couples are walking, separately, in Central Park on a warm summer night. One couple has a belief that walking in the park at night is dangerous. They're from out of town and remember reading about stories of muggings in the park. The other couple lives in New York City and has always believed that walking in the park at night is romantic.
>
> Suddenly a breeze blows and the bushes nearby begin to rustle. The couple with the belief that the park seems dangerous is triggered and experiences a wave of fear. They begin to walk faster and leave the park as quickly as they can.
>
> The couple with the belief that walking in the park at night is romantic experiences the breeze and the sounds of the bushes as a beautiful moment. They pause and embrace each other, then look up at the moon.

Both couples in our example felt the same breeze, yet their different beliefs shaped their experiences.

What Do We Really Believe?

Understanding that our personal tendencies spring from beliefs we have about ourselves is an important step on our journey. Why? Because, as we've seen, our beliefs shape us and affect not only how we act in the classroom but also how we experience life.

Looking inward to find our personal tendencies as well as the beliefs that underlie them is the beginning of the most deeply personal part of our journey to Teaching Mastery.

A Look at the Limiting Beliefs Working Beneath the Surface of Mary, Francine, and Brian

Mary, the teacher who shuts down her feelings, believes:

"I'm not sure that if I exposed myself to people they would like what they see."

Francine, the pessimist, believes:

"I'm not good enough. It's better not to try new things than to fail in front of everyone."

Brian, the "worker bee," explains:

"I've always found that the best way to become part of a group is to make myself useful, to be the hardest worker. I guess I believe that being myself isn't enough. I have to *do* stuff."

We may never know what happened along the way to cause Mary, Francine, and Brian to adopt these beliefs about themselves. However, it's important for them to realize that their personal tendency is a manifestation of a deep-rooted belief that they have about themselves. It's also important that each of them becomes aware of their personal tendency and how it's influencing their classroom experience.

Our tendencies and beliefs are deeply ingrained in us and often are difficult to discern. For some of us, it's the sting of failure or the trauma of a life-changing incident that helps us come face to face with our personal tendency. We call these incidents "breakdowns." It's almost as if the quiet inner teacher we've ignored for so long conspires to grab our attention by breaking into our life in a more dramatic way.

"Oh! You're not going to listen to my whisper? Well, maybe I'll have to *shout*!"

Tammy was in her third year of high school art and, more than anything, wanted to enroll in an advanced art program for her senior year. Her teacher, Mr. Brennan, refused her. She tried to reason with him and promised to put everything she had into the program, but he was adamant that she wasn't ready for it. Tammy was so hurt and upset that she quit school that very day and walked home.

The following year she graduated from a nearby high school and went on to college. Decades later, as an adult with her own children, she realized she was still holding on to the anger she had directed at Mr. Brennan. She wanted to apologize and forgive him so she could get on with her life, so she tracked him down. He was well retired, but once he realized who it was on the phone he became animated.

"Tammy, when you quit school it shook me up. It was because of you that I changed my entire approach to teaching. It was because of you that I changed as a person. You were the student who changed my life!"

Because of his breakdown with Tammy, Mr. Brennan woke up to his tendency to be rigid, inflexible, and unsympathetic. His new awareness changed him, though it was a painful, disruptive chapter for both him and Tammy.

Remember the angry incident with Mr. Jones and his student Marty in chapter 8? It was the teacher's version of a breakdown. After completely blowing his top, he felt awful about how he'd handled the situation and recognized that it wasn't the first time he'd lost control of his temper. His personal tendency had come to the surface before, but this time he'd made a real mess and knew he had to do something about it. He later commented:

I pulled Marty aside after class one day and apologized

for the way I acted, but it wasn't enough. I could see it in his eyes. I'd lost him. My behavior was understandable, but very unprofessional. I never realized how intimidating my flare-ups could be, and I never wanted it to happen again.

The problem with gaining awareness of our personal tendencies through traumatic incidents and breakdowns is that they generate a lot of pain and suffering for us...and for others.

Walking Down a Different Street

It might be helpful to think of our beliefs as mental constructs, not as facts. No matter how our beliefs came to be formed, they're merely thoughts that exist within our minds. In that sense, they're not real and therefore it's possible to change them.

For example, the Wright brothers had thousands of years of history and observable facts to prove the widely held belief that humans could not fly. They consciously chose, thankfully for us, to adopt the belief that flight was possible.

The Wright brothers turned on its head the old saying "I'll believe it when I see it." Their success is an example of *"You need to believe it, to see it."* We can *choose* what we wish to believe.

> Think what would happen if Mary, the teacher who shuts down her feelings, believed:
> "I'm a good person. I've got nothing to hide."
> Or if Francine, the pessimist, believed:
> "I'm a good person. Having things fall flat once in a while is part of being a creative teacher. It doesn't hurt to take a few reasonable risks."
> Or if Brian, the "worker bee," believed:
> "I'm a good person. I don't need to work so hard to prove myself."

Adopting a new set of beliefs that doesn't limit their view of the world and their classrooms would totally transform Mary's, Francine's, and Brian's teaching practices (not to mention their personal lives).

As we continue to explore our inner selves more deeply, we begin to see that what we believe about ourselves and who we are as individuals is fundamental to our classroom success. And, once again, we find ourselves at the intersection of the personal and the professional.

In sum, the limiting beliefs we have, whether conscious or unconscious, can undermine our best intentions and create personal tendencies that are riddled with self-fulfilling patterns of negativity.

> Perhaps the most important single cause of a person's success or failure educationally has to do with the question of what he believes about himself. —Arthur Combs

Being self-aware and gaining an understanding of our personal tendencies and the beliefs that underpin them are vital steps in the cultivation of our best self. We'll always have our tendencies; they'll never completely disappear; but they don't have to have an unbreakable grip on us.

Our present doesn't have to be ruled by the habits of the past. It's by noticing these habits and choosing to "walk down a different street" that we create a space for new, more-effective behaviors to emerge, and when we do that we're no longer captives of our past. We have a choice.

We're free!

REFLECTIONS

1. Over our lifetimes we've developed certain habits, automatic responses, historical patterns of behavior, and personal tendencies that are repeated unconsciously and that prevent us from choosing freely from the full range of actions available to us.

2. Our beliefs, tendencies, patterns, and automatic behaviors might have been useful for our psychological, social, or physical survival at one time, yet may not be serving us well now.

3. The beliefs that underlie our personal tendencies were absorbed, consciously or unconsciously, from our experiences, as well as from our family, friends, religion, school, community, and culture.

4. Some of our beliefs are limiting ("It can't be done!" or "I just can't do it!").

5. Our beliefs are mental constructs, not facts, and they affect how we experience life.

6. The less we are guided by our habits, automatic responses, historical patterns, and personal tendencies, the freer we are to take the most appropriate action in the moment.

ACTIONS

1. Which personal tendencies, historical patterns, or automatic behaviors can you identify? List them.

2. Examine each item on your list. Identify the beliefs that underlie each tendency, pattern, or automatic behavior. Are there any "limiting" beliefs? For any item that you've identified as a limiting belief, write a belief statement that would be more supportive of your purpose and calling.

3. Work with a trusted colleague or coach who can help you surface your tendencies and historical patterns. Ask them to let you know when they notice you engaging in them.

4. Try doing an Emotional Autobiography, as described in the *Practices* section.

5. Each time you catch yourself engaging in a personal tendency, historical pattern, or automatic behavior, reward yourself by putting a dollar in a cup. Later, use the cash to reinforce the changes you make.

The Journey

Above the mountains
the geese turn into
the light again

Painting their
black silhouettes
on an open sky.

Sometimes everything
has to be
inscribed across
the heavens

so you can find
the one line
already written
inside you.

Sometimes it takes
a great sky
to find that

first, bright
and indescribable
wedge of freedom
in your own heart.

Sometimes with
the bones of the black
sticks left when the fire
has gone out

someone has written
something new
in the ashes of your life.

You are not leaving.
Even as the light fades quickly now,
you are arriving.

— DAVID WHYTE

CHAPTER 10

RESILIENCE

Courage doesn't always roar. Sometimes courage is the little voice at the end of the day that says I'll try again tomorrow.
—Mary Anne Radmacher

It does not matter how slowly you go as long as you do not stop.
—Confucius

Beginnerhood

The journey to teaching mastery can be challenging and at times emotionally overwhelming. We feel confused, uncertain, and disoriented as the familiar mind, logic, and rational thought processes we've relied on to navigate through our lives gives way to new (and unfamiliar) instrumentation—our bodily sensations, our breath, the voice of our heart.

Learning to act in new ways and practicing new behaviors drops us into the role of beginner. No matter how long we've been teaching, when we change what we do in the classroom we're not seasoned veterans anymore; no, we're taken out of our comfort zone. It takes time and practice for us to make the transition from our old, familiar habits to the new, more powerful presence of the Master Teacher.

Mary (chapter 9), the teacher who tended to shut down her feelings, is now doing her best to adopt a new belief, thinking and saying to herself:

"I'm a good person. I've got nothing to hide."

When she feels the bodily sensations of anxiety that in the past would cause her to curb her emotions, disconnect from her students, and drop her voice to a monotone, she forces herself to ask a question or make an off-the-cuff remark. She deliberately works to fill her voice with energy.

Still, Mary's new behaviors feel phony and forced; and some days she goes back to her old, familiar monotone. When she realizes that she's slipped back, she gets upset with herself. Mary occasionally thinks, "I'll never get it." Her inner critic uses her missteps to reinforce her old beliefs about herself, such as, "See, you can't do it. There's something wrong with you."

Francine, who in the past didn't believe in herself and was afraid to fail in front of other people, is working on putting herself "out there" by taking a few reasonable risks. Inevitably, some of them fall flat and she feels like a fool. She thinks, "I knew this was going to happen. I'm not the creative, risk-taking type. How stupid of me to try."

Brian, the "worker bee," is practicing taking it easy. He's doing his best not to prove his value by working harder than everyone else. He keeps feeling drawn to volunteer for things and feels left out when he doesn't.

Each of our courageous teachers is experiencing the confusion and pain of the beginning learner. Yes, learning is often exciting and fun, but it can also be frustrating. It's good for us teachers to remember, now and then, what it feels like to be in the unfamiliar territory of "student." It's a place where we're no longer the confident experts. It's a difficult experience for those of us who are used to being good at what we do; yet experiencing the emotional ups and downs of the beginner is a great foundation for cultivating empathy and compassion—both key elements of the infrastructure of the Master Teacher.

Lapses and missteps are simply a natural and important part of the learning and growth process. So, when we feel our mood begin to darken and our frustration grow, it's a good time to notice how far we've come and then to celebrate it.

> Try looking at your mind as a wayward puppy that you are trying to paper train. You don't drop-kick a puppy into the neighbor's yard every time it piddles on the floor. You just keep bringing it back to the newspaper. —Anne Lamott[1]

For every few, tentative steps we take towards our goal, our new belief, or new behavior, there will be at least one disappointing slip backward. Our inner critic will be more than happy to emerge and berate us, by saying something like "You're not doing anything right!" or "You'll never get it! Just give up."

When we feel discouraged the last thing we need is to be hard on ourselves. What really helps is a little TLC. The best way to administer it is to cut ourselves some slack. After all, we're fallible human beings, not robots. We're not perfect and never will be, but we *can* learn to accept and love ourselves, as imperfect as we are.

> A group of young elementary school boys and girls are out on the playground shooting basketballs. The basket is ten feet high and to reach it these beginners must shoot with two hands because they don't have the the strength at their age to shoot one handed. Over time some of them become quite adept at shooting two handed. They can sink shots from anywhere on the court.
>
> When they get older they begin to play on organized teams. The coach shows them how to shoot one handed. It's essential that they learn this skill because as the level of competition they encounter increases they'll have difficulty shooting

with two hands, since it's just too easy to block that style of shot. Two-handed shooting is for beginners only.

So the youngsters begin practicing shooting one-handed, and, of course, they miss shot after shot. One-handed shooting feels odd and uncomfortable. They grow discouraged.

Each of them is much better at shooting with two hands, so whenever the coach isn't around, or has her back turned, a few continue to shoot two-handed. After all, it's more fun to make baskets than to miss them.

Those who continue to practice shooting one handed, even though they miss shot after shot, eventually begin to make a few baskets. Success builds on success, and over time most of them progress from minimally competent, to competent one-handed shooters. The two-handed shot is left behind. They've made it to the next level.

Unfortunately, those who continued to practice the old, familiar two-handed shot are eventually left behind.

Like our young basketball players we began practicing many of our behaviors when we were quite young. We're good at them, for the most part, and up to now they've served us well. Giving up what is familiar and known for a promise of mastery is especially difficult when the first steps we take aren't those steps of an expert, but those of a clumsy beginner.

Developing new behaviors and attitudes is even tougher if we're one of those folks who've been successful with our own version of the "two-handed set shot." It's very common even for well-respected educators to dismiss the possibilities of new and potentially more effective behaviors and approaches merely because, like our two-handed-shooting basketball players, they think, "If it ain't broke, why fix it?"

To make it through this difficult phase of learning, it helps to be especially patient with ourselves and maintain a tenacious dedication to our larger purpose and answers to the question "for the sake of *what*?" It's our larger purpose and calling that grounds and inspires us to embrace the uncomfortable feelings that come with new beginnings. It also helps to remember that this isn't just about us. We're also taking this challenging path for the good of our students.

By taking care of ourselves, we're taking care of them.

A New Voice

The journey to Teaching Mastery is a marathon, not a sprint. It's best not to rush things. Our heart—the voice of our inner teacher—is the wisest guide. It knows exactly how far we can run before we start to fade, and how fast. It's a patient voice and deserves our respect.

In the martial art Aikido there are a number of beautiful, but difficult, throws and falls. It takes quite a bit of practice to learn to do them safely. But some new students can't wait to fly through the air and land oh, so delicately; so they rush the process. They force themselves to overcome their natural fear of being hurt by launching themselves into falls that generally take years to master. More than one such student lands, let's say it nicely, *not so* delicately.

Forcing the issue can get one hurt on the mat, just as it can off the mat. It's best to take whatever time we need to feel comfortable with our new behaviors. Fortunately, we have an internal thermostat (call it homeostasis) regulating our emotional temperature and the constant tension between keeping the status quo and change. Too much change at once can disrupt our internal balance. But too *little* change can lead to stagnation. We need both.

It's okay to be cautious in our path toward changing our teaching style, just as long as we're not letting our fears hold us back. Yes, we'll continue to move forward and at times we'll have to assert our will; but all along the way we'll also be called to listen to our heart and to let things happen organically. As Mary Oliver writes,

> And there was a new voice
> Which you slowly
> Recognized as your own,
> That kept you company
> As you strode deeper and deeper
> Into the world.[2]

The voice of the heart—our inner teacher—is the starting point for many of life's great journeys. We understand this intuitively, and when we're able to stop the whirring and spinning of our minds for a moment, we begin to feel it. We feel our body and our center; we hear the "new voice" that has been secretly conversing with us throughout our entire life.

This new voice is our heart, whose familiar glow illumines the darkness and warms the chill...the heart that keeps us company as we stride deeper and deeper into the world...the heart that whispers its truth to us quietly, gently, always the patient one.

As we travel the path and take a moment to look up and see the stars beginning to burn through the sheets of cloud and the sky opening above us, we know that in order to grow there must be a letting go. And we know that the road to Teaching Mastery asks that we summon the courage to give more of ourselves, not less.

We're not leaving, we're *arriving*.

REFLECTIONS

1. In the process of breaking free from our habits, personal tendencies, historical patterns, and automatic behaviors, we'll occasionally slip back to our old ways.

2. Developing new behaviors puts us in the position of "beginners." There may be a period where we feel less competent then we did with our old behaviors.

3. It takes courage to leave behind the familiar practices of the past so we can step into new, unfamiliar ones.

4. If we are to succeed in the long run, we need to be resilient and extremely patient with ourselves. We simply can't let the negativity of our inner critic overwhelm us.

ACTIONS

1. At the beginning of each day, after you take a moment to state your purpose (look back at chapter 4), write one or two actions you intend to take that day to fulfill it. Doing this will help keep you focused and aligned with your larger purpose and intentions. It will also keep you from being hijacked by the day-to-day duties of your job.

2. At the end of each day, reflect and write a few brief sentences that summarize the steps you took to fulfill your declaration, and note any places where you feel you fell short. Like your morning declaration practice, doing this keeps the process of creative change from fading into the background.

3. Whether you've fallen short of your intentions for the day, or experienced some success, or a bit of both, simply notice without judgment, and then recommit. Take time to feel gratitude for what you've done, because simply doing this exercise at the end of the day *is* success. You're moving forward.

4. It helps to keep a daily journal so that you can track your progress.

Tim

Tim was my student. No, in truth, I was *his* student, for he taught me some of the deepest and important lessons I have learned in my life. Tim was a short boy, with shoulder-length, tussled brown hair. He was a loner, and unfortunately his ninth grade teachers and classmates treated him like an outsider. Tim showed little interest in school. He came from a poor family and his clothes showed wear and a lack of washing.

I had a long relationship with Tim. He was stubborn about not following the rules. If there was homework, he ignored it. If there was reading or studying to be done, he usually left it undone. Grades didn't motivate Tim. Punishment didn't deter him. School held no interest. Most of us (including myself, I am ashamed to say) treated Tim like a lost cause. We stopped thinking of him as a 14-year-old kid with a tough family life and looked at him as an obstacle to be dealt with, an object to subjected to the rules, punished, to be taught lessons—lessons that he, in defiance, chose not to learn.

I never understood how Tim looked at the world. I always have thought it harder to be defiant and stubborn than to "go with the flow." But whatever work Tim shirked he eventually ended up having to do. I never let that part slip. I'd make him do it for me after school, sitting alone, silently, bent over a blank sheet of paper in my classroom.

"Tim," I asked him half-heartedly, "wouldn't it be easier if you did this work the first time? You'd get the full credit for it and not have to stay after school. You always end up doing it anyhow." I knew my logic wouldn't break through his stubborn behavior; and, sure enough, Tim would give me a wan smile and merely shrug his shoulders.

The first lesson Tim taught me was the lesson of the limits of power. The school day was over. He had not read the chapter of *Adventures of Huckleberry Finn* that I had assigned the previous night for homework. So I seated him in my classroom, gave him a stern lecture, and ordered him to read the chapter he had not read for homework. Whenever I lectured him it somehow made me feel good, as if I was in control. I felt I had him; he couldn't hide from me, couldn't defy me.

Leaving Tim to his task, I walked out in the hallway and struck up a conversation with one of my colleagues. I deliberately stayed out in the hall to make Tim feel isolated in his punishment. When I eventually went to check on him, he was sitting back in his chair, legs outstretched...with...with...the book held, defiantly, upside down. I went ballistic and began to rush toward him in a rage. I had no idea what I was going to do when I got there; but I had snapped. He had pushed me too far this time. I felt as if he were slapping me in the face.

I was halfway to him, pushing desks and chairs out of my was as I went. He looked up at me just before I reached him. He showed no fear. In fact, his face had a childish grin on. It was a grin that Huck Finn or Tom Sawyer might have flashed during one of their adventures. Instantly, the grin struck me in a way that disarmed me. It was at once innocent and impish. It was a boy's grin—the grin of a real live, feeling, confused, 14-year-old boy.

I stopped in my tracks and for a moment saw the humor in the scene: a red-faced, spluttering teacher and this impish kid holding his book upside down. For some strange reason, I smiled back. The moment that I smiled, the two of us saw each other differently—not in our roles of angry teacher and problem student, but instead as fellow human beings. I could see in his eyes that Tim was as startled as I was by this strange encounter, this strange feeling. We were looking at each other as if for the first time.

Shaking my head I said, "Tim, what am I going to do with you?" We both kept smiling. "Go on, Tim. Go home."

Tim popped up from his seat and started toward the door. As he reached the threshold, he turned back for a brief moment. Our eyes met. "Mr. Reilly..."

I didn't let him finish, saying, "You're free, Tim. Go on, get out of here." I motioned as if pushing him away with my arm in feigned exasperation.

He turned and left.

After that day, Tim and I had a different relationship. I stopped looking on him as an obstacle. I stopped being so hard on him. My heart opened to him. Tim held a special place among my students. I would tease him in a good-natured, friendly way, and he always returned the favor. Every now and then he did his homework. He even wrote a poem or two before the end of the year, but there were still many afternoons spent in my classroom after school making up assignments, only now

I sat next to him and looked for openings to help him. He never shared much about his life outside of school. He wasn't much of a conversationalist.

I wish I could say that Tim turned his life around and that everything turned out well for him. When the year ended, he went on to other teachers in our school. But he was eventually ground up by the system. Each year things got tougher for him. Because of his reputation, he rarely got a clean start with a new teacher. He had fewer friends. He was worn down; I could see it in his face. Still, he defiantly refused to quit school.

Whenever I passed him in the hall or got a chance to say hello to him, I did. Looking back now, I can see he did his best to teach me how important having a big heart is for an educator. The kids who need the most love can make it awfully hard for us teachers to love them. I wasn't ready for his lesson then, though it was a seed that would blossom beautifully later in my life.

Tim was defiant, I eventually realized, because he felt powerless. He had been reaching out for me and for others his entire life. I didn't understand it until decades later. Tim was a beautiful boy, and taught me many things about myself. He was such a delicate soul.

Tim's father, I learned, was a drunk. One night before he graduated, his father took after him in a fit of anger. Tim decided he wouldn't submit to another vicious beating. He locked himself in the bathroom of the family trailer and, in a last act of defiance, took his own life.

I'm so glad I got to know Tim.

I miss him.

CHAPTER 11

PRESENT AND CONNECTED

*The greatest gift you can give (yourself
or anyone else) is just being present.*
—Rasheed Ogunlaru

External Awareness

Self-awareness doesn't end *within* us; it's merely a preparation for action. Action involves interacting with the world outside ourselves, our classrooms, our students. We move from the inside out.

When a baseball batter steps to the plate his first job is to center himself by focusing inward. He calms the chatter of his mind and blocks out the noise of the crowd. He reminds himself that he has a tendency to hitch his arm when he swings, so he creates a mental image of the new smooth and successful swing he's been practicing. If he notices he's nervous, he does his best to channel his excitement into power by relaxing the places in his body that feel tense. He reminds himself to breathe. All this is done in a few moments while the pitcher on the mound winds up to throw.

Preparing himself this way is not going to change the pitcher's actions or the speed of the pitch, nor will it guarantee a hit. The batter is simply bringing his "best self" to the plate and has prepared himself, in the instant, for whatever the pitcher decides to throw. Preparing ourselves this way gives us a greater chance of success, no matter what our endeavor—whether it be sports, or teaching.

Yet it doesn't end there. Once the batter has prepared (centered) himself, he brings his attention and awareness to what's going on around him. He may check to see how the infielders are positioned. Is the third baseman playing too far back? If so, maybe a bunt is in order? He may focus his attention on the pitcher's windup. Does he hold his glove a different way when he's about to throw a fastball? Noticing a small change in the pitcher's body, or glove position, may telegraph his intent, and that tiny bit of information can help the batter be extra-ready for the fastball.

When we work from the inside out we practice self-reflection, self-awareness, and self-preparation. That done, we can be more fully present, open, and connected to the emotional ecosystems of our classrooms and the needs, wants, and dreams of our students.

Being Present and Connected in the Classroom

We may think, "I'm *already* present and connected to my students." No doubt that's true for most of us, yet at the same time, just as there are different levels of self-awareness, there are different levels of presence and connection.

> Jennifer has a student, Maria, who has been frustrating her with yawns of indifference and unfinished homework. In her mind she's labeled Maria as "not caring," so she has come to pay a little less attention to her. After all, Jennifer has dozens of students in her class who need her attention and who *do* care.
>
> One day, after her last class, Jennifer approaches Maria and begins an innocent conversation with her. As the conversation progresses she listens carefully, focusing her full attention on her. As Maria speaks, Jennifer can feel her aware-

ness gowing. She begins to understand something new about her student. Jennifer realizes that Maria isn't indifferent, but fearful. She's terrified of failing and making mistakes in front of her classmates. She's so afraid of looking stupid that she doesn't try, and all the while she pretends she doesn't care.

Jennifer's problem student, whom she'd begun to pass over for more seemingly motivated students, was actually in need of *more* of her attention, not less.

As Jennifer discovered, there is seeing, and there is *seeing*.

A science teacher gave his students an assignment to go out and find a small, unnoticed flower.

"Use a magnifying glass," the teacher told his class, "and study the delicate veins in the leaves. Notice the nuances and shades of color. Turn the leaf slowly and observe its symmetry. And remember, this flower would have gone unnoticed and unappreciated if you had not found it, picked it, and admired it."

But the real lesson for the students came when the assignment was completed.

"People are just like that unnoticed flower, too," the teacher summarized the activity. "Each one is different, carefully crafted, and uniquely endowed. But you have to spend time with a person to realize this. So many people go unnoticed and unappreciated, because no one has ever taken enough time with or noticed their uniqueness."

Busy-ness

No news here: Teaching is a demanding profession. It can consume every minute of our workday, and often crowds our evenings, and weekends. There's so much to do and so little time to do it. We have classrooms full of students, each with unique gifts, needs, wants, and desires. Is it even possible to be present and connected to each of them? We say to ourselves, "Yes, connecting with each of my students is a good idea, but I'm just too darn busy. I simply don't see how it can be done."

> I stopped at the desk of Kelly, a shy, seventh grade girl who had written an essay about her favorite pet. It was Monday morning, and over the weekend I'd read and commented on 125 student essays that I had assigned my classes as homework. After handing out the corrected papers, I moved up and down the rows of desks, pausing to comment on an item or two with every student.
>
> I leaned over Kelly, who had struck me as rather shy, and began to point out grammatical and structural errors in her writing. My finger pointed to a misspelled word and then to a sentence fragment. Suddenly, right next to my finger a teardrop fell, smearing the blue ink. Before I fully understood what was happening, another tear fell, and then another. Kelly's head was down as she cried silently.
>
> A wave of awareness washed over me. Kelly had opened her heart and written about a beloved pet that had recently died. She had trusted me enough to share her loss, and in return I had totally missed it. I didn't mean to miss it, but when there are 125 essays to grade it's so easy to rush, to miss things.
>
> A tidal wave of sensations and emotions coursed through my body. Kelly, the sobbing child sitting in front of me, was not an abstraction or a test score. She was a real human being, and I had inadvertently broken her trust and hurt her feelings. From that moment on Kelly stopped putting forth her best effort in my class. She did what she needed to do, and no more. I never regained her trust.

My experience with Kelly drives home the enormous responsibility and power that comes with being a teacher. Obviously, it goes far beyond the curricula, the textbook, and bubbled answer sheets. Kelly's tears were a great personal lesson for me, but they also stand as a reminder to each of us about the importance of being fully present and attentive to our students—and of the consequences when we fail to be.

Slowing down just a little in order to notice, to offer a few words of acknowledgment or encouragement, can have a life-changing effect.

> "Kelly, I'm so sorry that your pet passed away," I wish I had told her. "I didn't know. You must have really loved him."

How we pay attention to our students will, of course, be unique to each of us, but understanding them as human beings has the potential to make an enormous difference in their success and ours.

When we're truly present—in mind, body, and heart—we see more clearly. We will be more aware of issues, like the mood of the class, that may have gone unnoticed in the past. We can develop a better sense of who in the class needs encouragement, motivation, and support—and how best to provide it.

> Unhurried, undistracted attentiveness is what teachers need in order to observe their students carefully, to know them well and understand how each one is making sense in the world. We talk about "meeting our children where they are" but, really, we can only do that if we *see* them, are attentive to them. —Teacher

So Many Distractions

When we're stressed out and overwhelmed, when we're distracted and thinking about what just happened, or what's going to happen next, our minds are in charge. We don't see clearly, because we're not fully centered or present in the moment. Gone is our self-awareness and inner wisdom. We might say we're "in our heads." We're experiencing the world only from the neck up. Whenever we do this, we severely limit our awareness of what's happening around us. We're like a distracted driver, speeding along on cruise control while lost in our thoughts. We can get so caught up in the whirlwind of our minds, our preparation, our content, and our agenda that we miss the daily opportunities we have to truly connect to the hearts of our students.

> A candidate for a teaching position sits in a conference room surrounded by a panel of teachers invited there to interview him. While they're waiting for the principal to arrive, the eager candidate scribbles away in a tiny notebook that sits open before him. This goes on for quite some time. He never looks up. He never engages the group. He's missing a great opportunity to chat informally, to allow the panel to get to know him, to build a little bridge of trust before the "real" show begins.
>
> The candidate clearly wants to do well. He probably thinks that preparing, and studying his notes, are keys to his success; however, doing that has just the opposite effect. By ignoring the interview panel and keeping his focus on his notes, by acting as if the panel were not in the room, he's turned them off. Without realizing it, he's bombed the interview before it's even begun. When the principal arrives, the panel goes through the motions of the interview but they're just being polite. There is no way they would consider hiring the aloof candidate.

Perhaps, given the importance of relationships and trust to the academic success of our students, we might consider a more structured approach to building them.

For example, if we're preparing a lesson on a short story, in addition to the key aspects of the story (theme, plot, symbolism, and so on), we might also include some affective planning that focuses on the following:

> Bringing some of our more-quiet students into the discussion
>
> Building the confidence level of some of our students
>
> Shifting the mood of the class if it's one of negativity
>
> Showing compassion and empathy for the students' struggles with the ups and downs of learning
>
> Recognizing and encouraging the strengths and gifts that we see in our students,
>
> Expressing gratitude for some aspect of their behavior or attitude.

The emotional, social, and psychological aspects of the classroom are foundational to successful teaching and learning. Do your students think school is a good place to be? Do they feel like they belong? Does each one feel you care about them? Do they feel safe? Supported? Special?

If the classroom environment isn't sound, learning will be difficult. So, in addition to reflecting on our own self, it's important that we deliberately focus on, and plan for, a healthy, affective classroom climate—one that is safe and trusting, and that elicits the best self, natural curiosity, and love of learning that exists in each of our students.

Looking Past Our Students' Exteriors

Creating a classroom environment that creates the conditions for our students' best selves to come forward can be extremely challenging. Not merely because of the busy-ness of our already overwhelmed schedules. It's difficult also because we're human beings and we tend to carry our positive and negative judgments and opinions about our students and our classes with us from day to day.

If we have a negative opinion of a student or a class lodged in our mind, it's difficult to build a positive, trusting relationship with that student or class. They may have clearly earned the negative assessment, but it gets in the way of our effectiveness.

> Think back to Jennifer, the teacher who had a negative opinion of Maria, a student who she thought didn't care about learning. It turned out that Maria *did* care but just didn't show it. If Jennifer hadn't become aware of this, she would have carried her negative assessment forward from day to day for the rest of the year and invested less of her time and energy in Maria.
>
> When Jennifer became more aware of what was beneath her problem student's veneer of indifference, her negative judgment vanished and she began to spend more time and energy with Maria, not less. Ultimately, Jennifer was able to build Maria's confidence to where she willingly stepped forward to participate in the life of the class. It was a great achievement for Jennifer—and Maria.

What would our classes be like if we were able, like Jennifer, to be centered and present enough to see our students with fresh eyes?

One of the most essential secrets of the Master Teacher is captured in Antoine de Saint Exupery's quote from his classic story *The Little Prince:*

> "Here is my secret. It is very simple. It is only with the heart that one can see rightly; What is essential is invisible to the eye."[1]

When we look past our students' exteriors and connect with their hearts, we're on the path to understanding them. Like icebergs floating in the vast Arctic Sea, they hide much of what concerns and motivates them below the surface. To be truly effective, we must learn to see the parts of our students that are "invisible to the eye."

Seeing the best self that often lies hidden within our students is far from easy. As we've discussed, the classroom is a complex organism composed of many individuals, each with their own set of experiences and each on a journey to find their own place in the world.

Sometimes the students who need us the most are the hardest to love. They seem to be at war with themselves, and they do everything they can to push us away. Their behavior is clearly self-destructive. Unfortunately, there are no simple solutions for breaking down the walls that some students build around themselves. Even so, it helps not to forget that there is something golden inside *every* student.

Michelangelo is noted for having remarked that inside every block of stone dwells a beautiful statue, and the sculptor need only remove the excess material to reveal the work of art within. Our challenge—a difficult one—is to be centered and present enough to recognize the beautiful work of art that is waiting to be discovered in each and every one of our students. Are we centered, present, and compassionate enough to work with the "excess material" that hides it?

Through the simple and deliberate process of bringing our attention first to our inner life and then outward to the life around us, we begin to experience new distinctions and fresh awareness. The powerful spotlight of our attention illuminates the classroom and our students in new ways. With our new awareness comes the ability to create greater levels of trust, compassion, and connection.

Research confirms the commonsense idea that when teachers' and students' agendas overlap and are in support of one another, we can create learning environments that are conducive to the highest levels of achievement.[2] If we choose to remain narrowly focused on our own agenda, no matter how important we feel it is, and if we merely pay lip service to our students' agendas, they'll find it difficult to trust us, follow us, learn with us.

It's good to remember that although content planning and preparation are extremely important, our finding success in the classroom has less to do with how smart we are or what we say than with the kind of person we are and how well we're trusted by our charges. No matter how much we prepare, if our students sense that we're ignoring them and the things they care about, they'll wake us up the only way they know how:

"Hey, you! Teacher! We're *people*! We count!
Pay attention to us! Wake up, Mister!"

REFLECTIONS

1. Attentiveness to our students builds our awareness of them and enhances their trust in us.

2. When we blend our agendas with those of our students' we create learning environments conducive to high levels of academic achievement.

3. The students who most need our attention are often the very ones who push us away.

4. What goes on in our classrooms ranges far beyond the curriculum.

5. The starting point for learning is the student.

ACTIONS

1. Assess your levels of attentiveness. On a scale of 1-10, how would you rate your level of attentiveness to your students? What objective criteria are there to support your assessment? How would your students assess your level of attentiveness?

2. Are there students in your class who tend to get less attention than others? Do you know why? List a few concrete ideas for being more attentive to them.

3. Have students fill out index cards that help you get to know them. You might want to know their plans when they graduate from school, their hobbies, their favorite subjects, and the like. Consciously use this information to build individual relationships with students over the course of the year.

4. Write what you think is the starting point for a particularly challenging student.

5. Create a Venn diagram of your most important agenda items, blended with your students' agenda items. Where can you find potential overlap?

6. Each time you develop a new curriculum lesson, write a brief plan that focuses on, and improves, the affective domain of the classroom.

7. Try the Clearing Negative Assessment activity in the *Practices* section.

Lost at Sea

I watched from the back of the room as a group of students began to disengage from their teacher. Several of them pushed their chairs back from their desks in frustration. They were lost. It didn't take long before they completely gave up on the lesson. They just couldn't keep up. The teacher was moving too quickly for them. I could almost hear them say, "What's the use!" A few short moments later, they began doing other, non-lesson related things at their desks.

I continued observing the class and noticed a number of individuals who were confused but hadn't yet given up. They were turning to neighboring students for help. At first it was just, "What did she say? I missed it?" But the teacher kept moving quickly and soon they were working with their neighbors as if the teacher wasn't even in the room. They'd figure this out together, it seemed

The majority of the class was trying to figure things out by themselves independently but seemed confused. Several students raised their hands for help. This slowed the teacher down. She stood near them, doing her best to figure out what they had done to get so lost, before she brought them back to where they were supposed to be.

The entire time the teacher was working with the lost "independents," there was a group of "high-end" learners who were totally bored because for them the lesson was painstakingly slow. They were getting angrier by the minute, and a few put their heads down on their desks in frustration.

Finally, there was a small but vocal group who was very angry with the class. Whenever they got lost they made comments like, "She's moving too fast. She should have been clearer...made the lesson simpler...provided more support materials." They spoke their criticisms loudly enough for the entire class to hear. They were the most angry and aggressive.

The class clearly was a mess. Even though the teacher was knowledgeable and well intentioned, the students were all over the place. It wasn't a pleasant scene—especially since *this was a class of school principals* learning how to use new laptops they had been issued a few days earlier. While there's no doubt the teacher leading the class could have been more effective, watching the assorted principals act out their frustrations in ways eerily reminiscent of their students was darkly humorous. It was obvious that they had completely forgotten what it was like to be beginning learners.

How different our classrooms might be if we remembered what it is to be a student...sometimes feeling "lost at sea" in a field of looming icebergs.

CHAPTER 12

THE IMPORTANCE
OF TRUST

*A lot of the conflict you have in your life exists
simply because you're not living in alignment;
you're not being true to yourself.*
—Steve Maraboli

Lack of Trust Impedes Learning

Even when we do our best to bring our self-awareness and heart to our
teaching, we can still meet a wall of rejection. Our students are not blank
slates. When they enter our classrooms they bring their own sets of experiences and background beliefs with them. Their experiences and beliefs influence how they perceive us and whether they're willing or even
able to trust us and connect with what we have to teach. Some of our
students have had negative experiences along the way (such as Kelly in
chapter 11) and Marty (chapter 9), which have damaged their ability to
trust. And interestingly, all our students are coming from a world where
there is much less trust of institutions, organizations, and authority.

Without positive relationships with us, or sometimes even with their
classmates, our students hold back and put their energy into protecting
themselves rather than into learning. Few risk stepping out of the shadows to engage fully in the learning process or in the life of the classroom.
Even if our students remain physically present in our classes, many drop
out mentally. Most do this passively, but a few become angry and
aggressive, doing everything they can to sabotage what's going on in

the classroom. The bottom line is that when there is distrust, student learning suffers.

We can get a better feel for what happens when trust is absent by examining its role in our teacher observation and review process. The official purpose for observing and evaluating us teachers in our classrooms is to provide feedback that will help improve our classroom practice. We're supposed to *learn* from the process; but if a building administrator enters our room to observe us and we have little or no relationship with them, many of us will play it safe and present a lesson that is tried and true rather than one that is more risky. After all, if the administrator doesn't know us and something doesn't go well, they might think we aren't competent.

The situation is even worse if we suspect the administrator doesn't have our best interests in mind or has a hidden agenda. In that case we become even more defensive and cautious. We'll receive feedback with suspicion because we aren't sure where the observer is coming from. In the worst case, if we feel the administrator isn't competent, we'll dismiss his or her comments out of hand. In each of the scenarios, the lack of trust allows fear to disrupt the learning process.

If we don't trust the administrator observing and later providing feedback to us, it's hard to put our entire heart into the process. This is also true for the students in our classes.

Trust Is a Perception

Trust is a highly valued commodity—and an extremely emotionally charged word. It's highly charged because it straddles both the professional and the personal. In the world of work, we trust others to get things done and to fulfill their commitments. We rely on colleagues to do what they say and we value people who are competent and reliable. Most, if not all, meaningful and lasting relationships are built on a foundation of trust.

If someone dares say they *don't* trust us, it hits us hard, striking at the core of our character. We're deeply insulted. It's a truism that, though we may have never been told directly, odds are that someone we know doesn't trust us.

Why are the odds high that we're not trusted by somebody? Recent research reveals that levels of trust in the workplace, not to mention throughout society, have fallen to all-time lows. A survey by Development Dimensions International underscores this sentiment—it found that 99% of employees think trust in the workplace is a vital need at work, but only 29% reported a high level of trust within their organization.[1]

There's an astounding disconnect between us, as individuals, feeling trustworthy and the reality of low levels of trust in the workplace (including our own classrooms). How is this possible? After all, aren't we well-intentioned educators driven by a calling to help others? We're honest and fair, and definitely not in the profession for the money. What's not to trust?

> Trust is "cultivated through speech, conversation, commitments, and action. Trust is never something 'already at hand,' it is always a matter of human effort. It can, and often must be, conscientiously created, not simply taken for granted."
> —Solomon and Flores[2]

The idea that trust "must be conscientiously created" is not the common sense. Many of us began teaching with the assumption that trust and positive relationships just "happen." After all, we've got good intentions and try our hardest to be fair with our students. Ultimately, however, it's our *students* who choose whether to trust us or not.

What's difficult for us to understand is that we can be extremely trustworthy, yet *not* be trusted, because no matter how we feel about ourselves, it's our students' perceptions that decide how much trust they give us.

In his book *Holding the Center*, Richard Strozzi-Heckler tells the story of working with an emotionally disturbed teenager with violent tendencies.[3] When Strozzi-Heckler asked him what he would like to learn, the teenager replied,

"How to kill someone."

It's a shocking statement and the common reaction would be to refuse the request, or to launch into a lecture about how learning to kill someone is not a civilized thing to do. Yet, by reacting with a sermon or with negativity, we'd go a long way toward closing the door to trust, and with it ending a relationship with the student. Strozzi-Heckler understood this. He knew there was more to learn and that it would take time for the troubled boy to trust him. He replied,

"I'll show you that...it's easy."

Accepting his student's request established a starting point for their relationship. It gave the teacher an opening. Once he had a place to begin, he was able to slowly and methodically build trust, and his relationship and connection with his student grew. Over time, the young man blossomed and his original request was no longer important to him.

Trust is the key element that steers the energy of teachers and students into achievement rather than disengagement and conflict.

Our students' academic success and personal growth are built on a foundation of trust, and it's the strength of our heart, our centered presence, and our personal attributes that are the keys to creating an environment where students feel safe, empowered, and connected to a set of mutual goals and values.

REFLECTIONS

1. Trust is a perception. Our students decide how much they trust us.

2. To build and sustain trust, we must consciously nurture it through our words and actions.

3. What we perceive as student indifference is sometimes fear, rooted in a lack of trust.

4. The foundations of trusting classroom relationships are the actual needs of our students.

5. When trust is lacking, teaching and learning are impeded.

ACTIONS

1. Identify and connect with one student who seems indifferent to learning. What's behind the indifference? What can you do to address the issue?

2. What would you anticipate your students saying is their greatest need, collectively? How can you address it?

The Power of the Spider

I was on the phone with my "teacher." The conversation had moved to an important crossroads. I was learning to open my heart more fully. At that moment, he said softly, "Look at that, a spider just appeared by the window." I was confused. What did this spider have to do with our work together? He continued, "Some Native Americans interpret spiders as having 'grandmother energy.' Grandmothers are so often touchstones of unconditional love." I immediately thought of my own grandmother and, like the petals of a delicate flower, my heart opened and I felt the unconditional love she had for me. It was an intensely emotional moment.

A few days later I spoke with my wife, a middle school math teacher, about what had happened. It might not have made complete sense to Liz, yet she listened intently. A month or so later, we were eating dinner and she told the following story:

"We were in math class today, and one of the girls saw a spider on the classroom floor and screamed. The kids nearest her jumped out of their seats to see it. In just a few seconds the entire class was up, probably happy to have a little incident to add some excitement to the day. They were definitely overreacting.

"Several of the boys approached the spider and there were shouts from the group to step on it. 'Kill it!' the kids were all screaming. One of the boys was happy to oblige; but before he could stamp on it, I said loud enough for them to hear, 'You know my husband says that spiders hold grandmother energy.' They stopped and looked at me. .What's that?' one of the girls asked.

I continued, 'Some Native Americans believe that spiders carry the energy of their grandmothers.' The class had a look of general confusion, and several students asked, 'Really?'

"I walked over to where the spider had stopped. One of the boys shouted, 'Don't kill it!' Another shouted from the back, 'Pick it up and put it outside!' At that, an entourage of students carefully worked the spider onto a piece of paper and the entire class escorted it to the window where they gently released it to the softness of early spring.

"We all stood watching to see what it would do and in seconds it disappeared from view. No one wanted to return to their seats. An odd mood had overtaken the class. We had moved from frenetic, middle school excitement to quiet pride. As if we had done something important and meaningful.

"Did they believe it was 'grandmother energy'? I don't know; but I know they'll never look at a spider again without having the thought pass through their heads."

As educators we take so much of our power for granted. For the most part, our influence ripples through the world and over the generations silently, unnoticed. Our lessons are seeds. They are blown on breezes far and wide. They are carried by lively little streams to rivers and oceans where currents move them to lands we will never see. Whether these seeds germinate in distant lands, or close to home, and whether they grow immediately, or wait for decades, our gift is nestled in the hearts of our students.

Remember the power of the spider. From lips to lips, from heart to heart, the gifts we bestow and the lessons we teach ripple through time and space.

CHAPTER 13

BUILDING TRUST THROUGH LISTENING

The first duty of love is to listen.
—Paul Tillich

Listening Builds Trust

Listening doesn't come naturally to most of us, and generally, what passes for listening is merely the art of giving the speaker the *impression* that we're listening. We nod, grunt, or give some other form of feedback to let the speaker know we're paying attention; but our minds are busy thinking about what we're going to say when it's our turn to speak, or making judgments about the speaker and what they're saying, or just daydreaming. After all, we have our own views to express, and our own stories to tell.

When we aren't listening and aren't focusing our attention, we are not truly present or connected to the speaker. So the door to trust, and to the possibility of developing a meaningful relationship, remains closed.

It's a strange behavior, because most of us like it when we're listened to. It feels really good when someone sincerely gives us their complete attention. We immediately get a sense that they care. It opens a pathway to our heart. When we teachers listen to our students with this kind of focus, we validate them as persons, *and* we begin to get a bit of insight into who they are and what makes them tick. Listening, without judging, analyzing, or spinning off into our own stories, is a powerful practice that quickly builds trust.

> I learned a great lesson from one of my colleagues. We were standing in the hall one day after school and he began sharing something personal about his home life that was clearly upsetting him. Several fellow teachers passed us on their way home, saying, "Hello" as they passed. Each time, even though my friend was speaking, I looked up and said, "Hi" back.
>
> Finally, after several of these interruptions, my friend stopped talking. I asked him to go on, but he responded, "You don't care. You're not listening to what I am saying." He was right, and I knew it immediately. I wasn't giving him my full attention. I was being rude. —Teacher

Centered Listening

There's another important lesson we can learn from Richard Strozzi-Heckler's encounter with the student who wanted to learn to "kill someone" (in chapter 12). *The starting point for most learning is not the needs of the teacher but those of the student.* And the quickest way to find the "starting point" for learning and to build trusting relationships with your students is to cultivate the discipline of listening.

Seek first to understand then to be understood. —Stephen Covey[1]

More than anything else, listening is really about focusing our full attention on the speaker. As we know from our mindfulness and centering practices, maintaining our focus and attention without being distracted takes a fair amount of discipline. Fortunately, by engaging in mindfulness and centering practices, we've been training our attention and honing our ability to focus. The practices of centering and mindfulness not only nurture our inner garden, creating conditions for our best self to emerge; they also create a space for the voices of others, such as our students, to be heard.

We can use the same process to build our listening skills, in which we focus our attention on the speaker rather than the breath. As with mindfulness and centering, when we become distracted, we bring our attention gently back to the object of attention—in this case, whoever is speaking.

Beyond Words

Centered listening is more than merely parroting back the speaker's words. It's a listening that discerns the tone, mood, and emotion with which the words are spoken. Sometimes students aren't willing or able to speak overtly about their feelings, needs, dreams, and desires. If we listen only to their words and fail to receive all the nonverbal sounds and signals, such as tone of voice and facial expressions, we may be missing the most important part of the communication. If we're going to build trusting relationships, in addition to literal interpretations, we need to listen to the feelings, emotions, motives, and circumstances behind the words.

> Steve, a high school science teacher, promises that if his students do well on the midterm exam he'll arrange a field trip to a local science museum. He forgets to reserve the bus and the field trip falls through.
>
> "It was an honest mistake," he explains to the class. His students moan and groan in disappointment but seem to accept the situation. Steve puts his mistake behind him and moves on but his class is still angry. Over the next few weeks the students become less enthusiastic, and the mood of the class sours. They feel that he's let them down, hasn't apologized sincerely, and should offer them an alternative reward.

But they never vent their frustration, and rather than dissipating it grows.

This class is a top group and the students keep their grades up, but for Steve and the kids class seems no longer fun. Some intangible thing has disappeared. Steve can feel that there's an issue but has no idea what it is. One day, he asks the class what's bothering them and is initially greeted with silence. One student speaks up tentatively, and that gives the others the courage to speak, and before he knows it, Steve has the entire class expressing their disappointment and frustration.

He's shocked at how hard the class has taken his broken promise. So he offers them a heartfelt apology and vows to come back to them with an alternative reward for their hard work. To his surprise, the apology breaks the negative mood and the class settles down. He's won them back for now, though he realizes that he's severely underestimated how important to their mutual success is his relationship with the class.

It's up us to use our centered listening skills to sense the undercurrents and moods that run in our classrooms and within our students' hearts. If our

> **You can improve your listening skills by trying the Attentive Listening activity in the *Practices* section.**

class is in a mood of anger or frustration (like Steve's), we would do well to take the time to shift its mood before moving to our own teaching agenda. When individuals or groups are angry, frustrated, or resigned, they're not interested in what we care about. They're too wrapped up in their own emotions.

However, once our students perceive that we're truly listening, when we acknowledge and understand their emotional state, and when they sense we really care about them, they'll be far more likely to allow us to move on to the things we care about (the classroom work). Being aware of our students' moods and consciously shifting them when needed opens new doors, builds trust, and creates opportunities for new and stronger relationships.

Secret Conversations

Our classrooms are full of secrets. We have ours, and our students have theirs. In each of our hearts there are secret dreams, quiet yearnings, silent fears...and always there are whispered doubts. Master Teachers cultivate hearts warm and strong enough to hear these secret conversations—both our students' and our own.

> Eduardo is pulled out of class by his teacher, Rebecca, because he's disrupting the class. In the hallway he breaks down crying, and says, "I hate people making fun of me. People are always making fun of me. They say I'm fat, and maybe I am, but that doesn't give them the right to tease me all the time."

Rebecca hadn't noticed the teasing and felt awful. Eduardo had hidden his pain well, for he always seemed to be confident and fun loving. The fact that he trusted Rebecca enough to reveal what was really going on, and the real pain he was suffering, was startling to her.

If it weren't for Eduardo's breakdown in the hallway Rebecca might have gone on disciplining him without ever understanding what was underlying his behavior. Because Eduardo trusted her enough to confide in her, Rebecca discovered that he was sensitive about his weight and had become the target of bullies. No matter how brave a face he put on, school had become unbearable for him. Armed with this new information she was able to take steps to curtail the bullying and make her classroom a more safe environment for all her students.

When you take the time to actually listen, with humility, to what people have to say, it's amazing what you can learn. Especially if the people who are doing the talking also happen to be children. —Greg Mortensen[2]

Yes, occasionally, we'll encounter students who'll want all our attention, all the time. Listening is a difficult task in itself, but it's even more difficult amid all the activity and energy of a class of lively students. It's not always possible, or even desirable, to shut out the entire class to give our attention to one student. When situations like those described above arise, we can let the student know that we care but we have other students and tasks to attend to at the moment. We can offer to meet and finish the conversation at another, more appropriate time:

> "Marcus, I want to hear the rest of this, but this isn't the best time. Why don't we get together at the end of the day?"

The important things to remember are that Marcus is important, that we follow through on the conversation, and that when we're able to listen we actually do.

If we ignore unspoken conversations, they fester and stand as impediments to trust, relationships, and learning. As we build trust and our relationship with the class grows, we'll find more opportunities to bring these unspoken issues to the surface, for we surely know they won't go away on their own.

Students yearn to be heard and to be understood, even those who are too shy or too disengaged to speak. Listening to what is being communicated by their words, their tone, even their silence, is an important element of our fully understanding the "person."

> The most basic of all human needs is the need to understand and be understood. The best way to understand people is to listen to them. —Nichols and Stevens[3]

REFLECTIONS

1. Listening is consciously giving our full attention to someone else.

2. Listening builds trust quickly.

3. We can learn to be better listeners through practice.

4. Centered listening discerns not only words but also tone, mood, and emotion. Sometimes unspoken conversations are going on that we need to surface so that we can create the right environment for learning.

5. We build trust by seeking to understand before being understood.

ACTIONS

1. Commit to improving your listening skills. Develop a practice of centered listening. Try the Attentive Listening activity in the *Practices* section.

2. Listen to the tone, mood, and emotions of your students when they speak. How would you assess the mood of your class? What criteria support your assessment? Is the mood negative, positive? indifferent? Why is it that way? What might you do to shift a negative mood?

3. Are there individual students in your class who would especially benefit from being listened to? Create opportunities for you to listen to them.

Teacher's Prayer

Lord, please help me
To strengthen their voices,
bodies and minds,
To express their feelings and
control them sometimes,
To explore what's near
and venture afar,
But most important to love
who they are.

—Author unknown

CHAPTER 14

BUILDING TRUST
THROUGH AUTHENTICITY

Trust is confidence born of two dimensions: character and competence. Character includes your integrity, motive, and intent with people. Competence includes your capabilities, skills, results, and track record. Both dimensions are vital.

—Steven Covey

Follow Through

While focused listening opens the doors to trusting student relationships, it doesn't take much for us to destroy them. A recent Harvard Business School study found that approximately 65% of American workers don't trust their management.[1] The most common reason respondents gave for this surprising lack of trust was:

> Managers say one thing and do another.

Whether we have good intentions, or there are extenuating circumstances, when we don't follow through on our commitments, or when our actions fall short of our words (especially if this happens more than once), we erode the trust that students have in us, or we make it difficult for trust to develop at all. Even if we're highly competent and enthusiastic, if we show up as unreliable we'll be assessed as untrustworthy.

Character

To be trusted we must "walk our own talk" and speak and act in ways that are consistent with what we say.

> A superintendent kicks off a new school year with an administrative retreat. Before he is one minute into his well-written remarks, the faces of his administrative team show they are tuning him out. Although he's delivering an inspirational narrative about bringing the district to "world class" status, his past actions don't align with the vision he's presenting. His team assesses him as inauthentic because he often changes his positions, based on which way the wind is blowing. Behind closed doors they refer to him as a "politician," and they don't mean that in a good way. His overall presence doesn't embody commitment.

Though the superintendent is an excellent speaker and says the right words, on more than one occasion in the past he's said one thing and then done another, eroding the trust of his administrative team. No matter how inspiring his words, he can't fake his personal integrity or hide his past track record. His staff questions his authenticity.

It's not what a person says or promises but their way of being in the world that affects whether others follow.

In large part, authenticity is about aligning our purpose, values, and beliefs (what we think and say) with our actions (what we actually do). In the classroom, our students, like the superintendent's administrative team, hear much more than our words; they hear the real intent and emotion behind our words. They sense our moods. They gauge our competence, dependability, and ability to keep them safe. They see beyond, and through, our "teacher" role, and it's not uncommon to find that their perception of us may not be the same perception we have of ourselves. Amazingly, they do much of this "perceiving" without being consciously aware that they're doing it.

Aligning Words with Actions

Many of the practices introduced so far are meant to help us cultivate and embody our best and most authentic "self." When our intentions, our words, and our actions align, and when we speak and act with real commitment from a foundation of "center," we can't help but exhibit a strong and inviting classroom presence. We're living in the sweet spot of our power, and our students perceive us as competent, consistent, sincere, and transparent. In short, they trust us.

> A teacher tells her class that they must be lifelong learners and risk takers if they want to be successful in life. She works hard to embody these characteristics herself. When she makes mistakes, or tries something new that doesn't work, she admits it. If she can, she also points out what she learned from the experience.

This teacher's students appreciate her honesty and authenticity. By modeling the behavior of a lifelong learner she makes it easier for them to take risks in her class. She's made it safe to fail. They trust her.

By contrast, when our words say one thing and our actions and body language say another, our students perceive that something is "off." They can sense our inconsistency and, in the worst case, our hypocrisy.

> Mr. Malloy, the middle school principal, welcomes parents to the "Moving Up" ceremony by sharing with the audience in a lifeless monotone:
>
> "I'm so excited to be here."
>
> The words he speaks and what he actually communicates couldn't be more disconnected. His monotone overwhelms his words. The audience doesn't hear the "excitement" but rather a tone that says:
>
> "I am performing a duty required by my position."

We can't successfully fake authenticity, although some, like Principal Malloy, try. After all, much of what we communicate in the classroom is not spoken in words but is conveyed through our unconscious body language and tone of voice. Our body conveys and betrays more than we realize about our true feelings.

Any parent who has forced a reluctant child to apologize knows there is a tone of "I'm sorry and I mean it," and a tone of "I'm doing this to get him [or her] off my back." It's similar to the way animals sense the real intent of our voice when we give them a command. We might ask our dog to get off the couch in a tone of voice that elicits nothing but a raised ear, or we might say it and really mean it, and the dog gets off the couch. There's something in our tone and bodily presence that says, "He's serious" or, in the former case, "He's not serious."

> Ellen is a busy teacher who prides herself in finding time to speak with her colleagues at work. She appears at the threshold of a classroom and asks the occupant how things are going. She never enters the room. It feels as if she's on her way somewhere else.
>
> Sensing her inauthentic presence, her colleagues generally give her a superficial response. Unconsciously, they perceive she doesn't really want to know how things are going. Her body placement and energy are saying, "I'm interested; but not *that* interested."

Ellen's colleagues pick up on the subtle disconnect of her body language, her words, and the partial offering of her attention, and they react by engaging in polite chitchat and nothing more. This is done not consciously but intuitively. Most of Ellen's communication is being done nonverbally and below the level of consciousness, and so are her colleagues' reactions.

An authentic person is one who is comfortable in their own skin, neither acting nor playing a role. There is little daylight between what they believe, what they say, and how they behave. This is the part of trust building that involves our character, our heart, and the best self we've been cultivating.

The Courage to Be Ourselves

We know authentic people when we meet them, but it's a rare occurrence. Why? We hide our true selves for many reasons, but let's consider one: fear, perhaps the fear that we'll be rejected, taken advantage of, laughed at, or shunned, or just plain fear of failure. When we're afraid, we close down and hold parts of ourselves back. We act in ways we think others will like. We're cautious, wondering what others are thinking about us.

Of course, a certain amount of social anxiety is to be expected. After all, wanting to be part of a social or cultural group is part of the human condition. It's woven into our ancestral DNA. We need others to survive. Yet the paradox is that the more we act the way we think others will like, the more we hold back and protect our hearts, the more difficult it is to build the relationships we crave. Being ourselves is one of the most difficult challenges we and our fellow teachers face on the road to Teaching Mastery, but it's essential if we're to earn the trust of our students.

The privilege of a lifetime is to become who you truly are.
—C. G. Jung

Courage is rarely mentioned as a component of the Master Teacher's personal infrastructure. The word's etymology, from the French root "cour," means heart. It truly takes a lot of heart, and a good deal of courage, for us to come out of hiding and let our authentic self be seen by others.

Tom is an experienced and enthusiastic teacher who tells the story of starting the new year committed to teaching more authentically, from his "heart." It's totally new territory for him. His classroom has always been highly structured and scripted, his own role being that of a benevolent dictator. It has always worked for him. He's never had any classroom management issues, and his students usually do well on the state tests. Tom felt he was ready to try a new, more free-flowing, creative style of teaching.

Tom relates that when he stood in front of his class on the first day of school, his heart was pounding as if he were a first-year teacher. He was surprised at how stressed out he was, and at the moment of truth he looked at his students and clung to his old way of teaching with all the fear of a first-time skydiver having a panic attack at the jump door of the plane.

Tom was feeling the fear and anxiety of letting go of his script. He may have been an experienced and successful teacher, but he wasn't used to letting more of himself—his heart—enter his teaching. The anxiety and confusion he felt was normal, and similar to the anxiety and fear our students feel when they're learning something that's unfamiliar to them.

Tom says, "Each morning before class I wrote my intention for that day in a journal. Doing this helped reinforce my commitment to changing the way I was teaching. It gave me a bit more courage to keep trying. I also doubled up on my mindfulness practices. I did a ten-minute session before I left home in the morning and another one at school during one of my prep periods. I can't think of a better way to prep for class.

"My practices helped me relax, and when I became uncomfortable and anxious, I'd just remind myself to slow down and breathe. Eventually I got past being a beginner and became quite good at teaching from the 'heart,' which for me was about letting go and being more myself. The feedback from my kids was great. They were learning and having fun. More than one student stopped to tell me everyone was enjoying the new me."

As the self we're cultivating grows, we can feel the powerful gravitational pull of our old self holding on, because the falling away of parts of ourselves can be traumatic. In a sense, we're saying our last good-byes to an old friend who has been very dear to us.

> *One doesn't discover new lands without consenting to*
> *lose sight of the shore for a very long time.*
> —André Gide

It's as if this part of our journey has led us to a tunnel we must walk through in order to reach our goal. It's a tunnel that curves through a mountain, so we can't see the light from the other side. We enter guided by the bright sun pouring in through the opening behind us, and as we walk deeper into the tunnel the opening gets smaller and the light grows dimmer.

Eventually, the light from behind us is no longer strong enough to illuminate our way, and the curve of the tunnel obscures whatever daylight is coming from the other side. We find ourself in the dark (like Tom), wondering if we've made a mistake. "This is scary," we say to ourselves "I could get hurt. What if this is a dead end? There must be an easier way to do this. I'll do it another time. I'm not ready yet."

Most meaningful endeavors bring us to the edge of our competence and comprehension. But if we have the courage to trust ourselves, walking in the dark, taking the next step, and then the next, continuing our practices, without knowing exactly where the path will lead us, eventually we'll see a pinprick of light that becomes larger and brighter as we move toward it. We'll emerge from the tunnel a slightly different person from the one who entered it.

"Does it hurt?" asked the Rabbit.

"Sometimes," said the Skin Horse, for he was always truthful. "When you are Real you don't mind being hurt."

"Does it happen all at once, like being wound up," he asked, "or bit by bit?"

"It doesn't happen all at once," said the Skin Horse. "You become. It takes a long time. That's why it doesn't happen often to people who break easily, or have sharp edges, or who have to be carefully kept."

—Margery Williams, *The Velveteen Rabbit*[2]

REFLECTIONS

1. Walking our talk builds trust. Our students and colleagues perceive us as authentic when our actions (not merely our words) align with our purpose, values, beliefs, and goals.

2. Students can detect when our words and behaviors aren't aligned.

3. All the best and worst parts of our personality are on display in the classroom.

4. It takes courage to be ourselves.

5. We can't compartmentalize elements of our personality. Eventually they show up in the classroom. We have only one self.

6. The voice of our heart is our most authentic self.

ACTIONS

1. Assess your authenticity. How aligned are your actions with your beliefs, values, and goals? Are you taking steps to fulfill your declaration? Are there areas where you might be out of alignment? What criteria support your assessment?

2. How would your students assess your authenticity? Make a list.

3. Think of your students as mirrors. What are their actions reflecting back to you? Are there lessons you can learn from them?

Working Together

...We shape our self

to fit this world

and by the world

are shaped again.

The visible

and the invisible

working together

in common cause,

to produce

the miraculous...

—DAVID WHYTE

CHAPTER 15

Stress and the Body

Your body is an absolute mirror of your mind. As you worry, your body shows it. As you love, your body shows it. As you are overwhelmed, your body shows it. As you are angry your body shows it. Every cell of your body is being allowed or resisted by the way you feel.

—Esther Hicks

Holding Stress in the Body

Our habits, automatic behaviors, historical tendencies, and the way we react when we feel stressed out are not simply provinces of the mind but real physical events. As we go through life, especially life in the classroom, we're bound to collect our share of psychological and emotional bumps and bruises. While most of these heal quickly, sometimes an unexpected classroom incident, or the general stress of the job, sticks with us and transfers directly to the muscles of the body.

Chronic stress is a major contributor to a litany of negative health issues. When we're stressed, we're more likely to experience headaches, backaches, stiff necks, stomach issues, and on and on. Our immune system dips and we're more susceptible to the common cold and flu. Unless we take steps to reduce chronic stress, our quality of life, both in and out of the classroom, will be less than optimal. It can also lead to a severe case of teacher burnout.

[U]nconscious tension causes changes in the body's nervous system. These changes include constriction in blood vessels and reduction of blood flow to the various soft tissues, including muscles, tendons, ligaments, and nerves in the back. This causes a decrease in oxygen to the area as well as a buildup of biochemical waste products in the muscles. In turn, this results in muscle tension, spasm, and back pain experienced by the patient. —William W. Deardorff, PhD, "How Does Stress Cause Back Pain?"[1]

The particular way our muscles contract when we're stressed and anxious causes our body to take on a shape, like clenching a fist. Our shoulders may creep up around our ears as we tense the muscles of our neck. We may become slightly bent forward, or bent to either side, as the muscles of our lower back become rigid and tense. Our shoulders may round forward as our chest muscles tighten to protect our heart. The muscles of our jaw can tighten, or our chin and lips contract, and it's not uncommon for our breathing to become extremely shallow. Over time, our bodily shape, like our behavioral patterns and tendencies, becomes our lived history—a manifestation of the state of our inner self. Our body is a reflection of our authentic self.

Dissociation

When we hold tension and stress in our body, we also tend to block out, or dissociate from, the uncomfortable feelings and the bodily sensations that are causing the anxiety.

In response to trauma, a common defense mechanism of the human body is dissociation—a disconnection—from...important forms of connection: self, others, and the surrounding world. The problem arises when we get stuck in dissociation after the traumatizing event has passed, no longer able to engage life fully.

Many of the victims of the earthquake in Haiti, with whom I worked, reported that they were unable to feel any sensations in certain parts of their body. This was a symptom of a possible ongoing dissociation. When our body is numbed such that we cannot feel pain, we are simultaneously deprived of enjoying the pleasurable sensations in our body.

When...we help people reconnect with their body and discharge excess traumatic energy, we are also helping them to expand their capacity to feel positive sensations...[and] help each person to reconnect with self, which, in turn, allows him or her to be more fully present to others and the world around them. —Fr. Dennis Moorman, "Haiti, Trauma, Spirituality and Somatic Experience"[2]

While we may never experience classroom trauma on the scale of an earthquake, even the minor stress- and anxiety-producing situations we encounter daily can cause us to shut down the feelings and sensations that seem so uncomfortable. When we dissociate, we constrict our emotions, just as we constrict our muscles. Shutting down our feelings of anxiety and stress, while holding, contracting, and tightening our muscles, is a type of "armoring." Over our lifetime, "armoring" shapes us both emotionally (our personal tendencies) and physically (how we hold ourselves).

The sensations that travel through us, or erupt within us, are sometimes so intense that they're frightening. We turn away from them lest they overwhelm us and dissociate by taking refuge in our minds. Cognitive thought can be a safe place where we can have wonderful insights that are intellectually pleasing, while shutting down the feelings and sensations of an awkward moment, the confusion of a free-flowing discussion, or the intimacy that breaks through our professional role and puts us in a more human and more vulnerable position.

When we dissociate from our body and our feelings, we aren't centered. Shutting down our feelings, and contracting and holding stress in our body, restricts our ability to be self-aware. In this state it's difficult to be present, open, and connected to our students, making it difficult to create trust and build relationships with them.

Shapes and the Perceptions They Create

Here are a few examples of how our bodily shape can influence how our students perceive us:

> Francine (in chapter 10) is a pessimist who believes that whatever she tries is inevitably going to fail. Her body reflects her negativity by her tendency to dip her head and look down at her feet when she is talking to the class.
>
> Perception: Her lack of eye contact communicates that she doesn't believe in herself or what she's saying.
>
> Tony, a teacher who tries very hard to be liked, tends to slouch, lean, and stand on one leg or another when teaching. He rarely stands erect, centered, and on his own two feet.
>
> Perception: His posture makes him look weak and ungrounded.

Mary's Journey

Is it really possible to cultivate the self by changing the shape of our body? Can our body take on and sustain new, more effective shapes?

Remember Mary (also in chapter 10)? She's the high school teacher with a historical tendency to shut down her feelings and hide her emotions when she's anxious. Observing her from the back of the classroom, one clearly sees this tendency in her posture. Mary's shoulders are rounded forward and her chest is curved inward, as if she were protecting something...perhaps her heart.

As part of her professional and personal development work, Mary is assigned a de-stressing (and reshaping) practice designed specifically for her. She is invited to lie on the floor, place a rolled towel between her shoulder blades, and let her shoulders relax. The towel forces her chest upward and out, as her shoulders roll back to touch the floor. While she's in this position she puts her attention on her breathing and her heart. Mary says,

> "It was uncomfortable at first. I felt like my chest was stretching like a rubber band. I had no idea how tight I'd become in that area. What surprised me even more were the emotional changes that started to show up unexpectedly. One night after practicing I was watching a movie on TV and for some reason I began to cry. I wasn't sad or happy; it must have been a release of some pent-up emotion or just the letting-go of the stress I'd been holding. It was strange, but it felt good.

> "I kept up my 'chest opening practice,' and as the school year went on I began to notice a difference in how I approached my students. I began to let down my guard and have little conversations with them, and eventually I began to feel their trust in me grow. It's funny how the more I opened up, the more they trusted me, and the more they trusted me, the more I opened up.

> "Now that I've opened my heart, I've noticed more students coming to me after school and even during their free periods for help. I'm getting more out of them in class, too."

Mary is a wonderful example of how by de-stressing, de-armoring, and reshaping our body we can unlock emotions, and parts of ourselves, that have been held in chronically contracted muscles for years.

Our shape affects the world and the world affects our shape.
This shape is our lived, felt experience that produces both a
worldview and an identity in the world.
—Richard Strozzi-Heckler[3]

De-stressing

The idea that the shape of our body influences how we think and feel, and how others perceive us, is not a common notion. As we've traveled the path to Teaching Mastery, we've learned to focus our attention and awareness on the body's breath, its moods and emotions, and the myriad of sensations that flow within it. But we can also cultivate ourselves by de-stressing, de-armoring, and reshaping our bodies.

> **I've included a Trying on Different Shapes activity in the *Practices* section.**

There are many practices designed to bring our body into shapes that release the muscle contractions caused by stress, anxiety, and the constriction of natural energy that these "muscle dams" create. Massage, yoga, tai chi, Aikido, and other martial arts, as well as acupuncture, are just a few of the more popular approaches to cultivating the self by reshaping and opening the body.

Although each of these disciplines is unique, all provide practices that allow us to relax and open "armored" muscles and chakras that have been in various states of chronic or semi-chronic contraction. As historically tense muscles open, like clenched fists unfolding, our shape begins to change and the physical aches and pains related to our stress begin to diminish.

When the energy and excitement (produced by our anxiety and stress, choked off and concentrated in specific muscles of our body) begins to flow freely, we begin to feel again. We're no longer dissociated from our body or our emotions. We become more present, authentic, and *alive*!

Our students perceive us differently, and it's easier for us to build trust and relationships.

> "The sun shines not on us but in us. The rivers flow not past, but through us, thrilling, tingling, vibrating every fiber and cell of the substance of our bodies, making them glide and sing." — John Muir

When we break free of our historically constricted shape, we also break free of some of our historical behaviors and patterns. Our muscles aren't as set and rigid, and our new flexibility of body allows us to experience the world from fresh perspectives. We feel shifts in our mood and emotions. Our body, our mind, and our emotions are more integrated. No longer dissociated from these parts of ourselves, we're more present and able to take new and more effective actions when we encounter stressful classroom situations.

Jane

Principal Jane thinks of herself as a forward-thinking educator. The door to her office is always open. She readily embraces new notions of teaching and learning, believes in empowering and engaging students and teachers, and works hard to bring technology to her school. Jane is clearly doing her best to bring about transformative change. Observing her, one would say she has her eyes on the horizon.

Occasionally, during the school year, Jane's responsibilities and commitments peak and she becomes overwhelmed with work. When Jane is under this type of stress, she retreats to her office, closes the door, and sits bent over her desk to do paperwork. Her eyes are no longer on the horizon and her vision shrinks to the size of the surface of her desk.

When Jane's body (and emotional) shape shifts from "eyes on the horizon" to "eyes on the desk," she looks submissive, unsteady, and weak.

She seems to disappear, and her staff perceives her as an inconsistent advocate for change. Initiatives stall out because her energy isn't sustained when things get stressful.

For Jane to be the leader she wants to be, she needs to embody a shape that consistently communicates her commitment to change. She has to keep her eyes up and on the horizon, and to stand in a way that is grounded yet connected to the future she envisions. To do this, she develops a new, personal practice designed to reprogram her tendency to fade away at stressful times. Whenever she feels compelled to close her door, she notices what she is feeling, pauses, and walks to a classroom in the building to observe a class for a few minutes.

Physically stepping into and facing the world, when her natural tendency when stressed is to step away, begins to change Jane's entire persona. Her staff notices the change, and one day a teacher stops her in the hall and asks if she's been working out or taking spin classes because she looks so much stronger and healthier.

Reshaping our body allows us to break free of long-held historical patterns of behavior and to experience our classroom in new ways. Working with the body is a radical departure from the notion that our rational mind can untangle all our tough problems.

It's by fully occupying our body, as well as our heart and mind, that we become one authentic and integrated "self."

We become whole!

REFLECTIONS

1. We hold stress and anxiety in our muscles. This can affect our physical and emotional health, as well as our bodily shape.

2. Our inner state is reflected in our body. Our body is our lived history.

3. Our shape can limit our physical, emotional, and behavioral range.

4. De-stressing, de-armoring, and reshaping the body can help free us from historical patterns, tendencies, and automatic behaviors.

ACTIONS

1. How would you describe your body shape? (Not as "tall/short," or "heavy/thin," but as hunched, tight, loose, grounded, flexible, rigid, aloof?)

2. Identify the place(s) in your body where you hold stress and anxiety. How would you describe the sensations you feel in this location?

3. How is your inner state manifested in your body?

4. Engage in an activity meant to de-stress, de-armor, and reshape your body. (Examples are tai chi, bodywork massage, yoga, acupuncture, and Aikido or another martial art.)

The Laughing Heart

your life is your life

don't let it be clubbed into dank submission.

be on the watch.

there are ways out.

there is light somewhere.

it may not be much light but

it beats the darkness.

be on the watch.

the gods will offer you chances.

know them.

take them.

you can't beat death but

you can beat death in life, sometimes.

and the more often you learn to do it,

the more light there will be.

your life is your life.

know it while you have it.

you are marvelous

the gods wait to delight

in you.

—Charles Bukowski

CHAPTER 16

Gifts and Gratitude

Let others see their own greatness when looking in your eyes.
—Mollie Marti

*Gratitude can transform common days into thanksgivings,
turn routine jobs into joy, and change ordinary
opportunities into blessings.*
—William Arthur Ward

Building on Our Strengths

As I left the Aikido dojo I turned to Firestone Sensei, who was busy watering a beautiful orchid set on the windowsill, and asked,

> "Next time I come, would you watch me do my backward roll and tell me what I am doing wrong? I'm having a hard time rolling on one side."

He answered immediately with a good-natured grin that is his hallmark.

> "Understanding what's missing won't help you learn how to do a backward roll correctly. Pay attention to what you're doing correctly on the right side and then practice it on the left."

His words were so simple and so, so true. They were a stark reminder that working with our strengths, not just shoring up our weaknesses, is an important part of our road to Teaching Mastery. Much of our attention and energy in schools is devoted to dealing with what is missing, and too little with what is actually there. When we think back to the teachers who have had the greatest effects on our lives, it's not surprising to find that most of them were the ones who recognized our strengths and our gifts, and who encouraged us to bring them into the world. As educators, "paying this forward" may be the best preparation for life we can give our students.

> *A child may be born with a talent but someone, such as a teacher, needs to realize and believe in it or it may not ever be nurtured. A teacher has the ability to reinforce, support, and appreciate both the work and the play of her students.* —Anonymous

Our gifts are often visible early in our lives. Mrs. Woodruff, my fifth grade teacher, pulled me aside after class one day and complimented me on an essay I had written on Civil War General Stonewall Jackson. She felt I had a talent for writing and asked me to be the editor of a class newspaper she had been wanting to publish. Her acknowledgment and her offer filled me with an emotion that's difficult to explain decades later. Yes, there was pride, but it was something more. I felt like the "real" me had been found, for I had been writing little stories and poems in secret for years. We only produced a single blue-ink, mimeographed issue of that class paper, yet Mrs. Woodruff's acknowledgment and support for my gifts put much-needed wind in my sails and helped give me the confidence to use my gift to write more often and more publicly. I think of her as one of the teachers who changed my life.

Focusing our attention on our students' strengths and gifts doesn't have to take a great deal of time. Like the science assignment described earlier (in chapter 11) about intently studying a flower, we're asked to notice what stands out, what seems to be at the heart of who our students are.

When we recognize our students' innate gifts, we're connecting with their essential core. Discovering their gifts is different from acknowledging their skills, because gifts, in our context, are innate, natural endowments. They come from the inside out. Skills, on the other hand, come from the outside in. They're learned. It can be difficult to tell the difference between the two. One teacher put it this way:

> I'd say the main difference is that working hard using my skills leaves me tired and drained, but working hard using my gifts leaves me tired and fulfilled. —Teacher

One of our challenges as teachers is to connect with and use whatever gifts we have. Some of us have been hammering away at our perceived shortcomings for so long, focusing on what we think is missing, that we've never fully explored our strengths and our gifts.

Few things are sadder than a gift gone undiscovered or a gift ignored. All gifts may not evolve into careers, and some never become more than beloved avocations. But whether it be career or hobby, as teachers engaged in the work of the head and the heart, we seek to recognize and encourage our own gifts and the gifts of our students, for we know that...

> always this energy smoulders inside
>
> when it remains unlit
>
> the body fills with dense smoke.
>
> —DAVID WHYTE[1]

When we use our gifts, we experience the fullness of our potential. Gifts are like seeds: Without nourishment they lie dormant, but we can bring them to life with the power of our heartfelt attention and our encouragement. Working with our students' strengths allows us to tap into their natural passion, motivation, and creativity. When we cultivate their gifts we connect to their hearts, their spirits, and their own "calling" and larger purpose. For us teachers, having a heart that's present and open—one that nourishes the gifts of others—is one of the most important, joyful, and rewarding parts of our work.

To assist another person on their life's journey is a weighty responsibility. Like humble gardeners, we must understand ourselves in order to tend to our students, those young seedlings growing in our classrooms. Some students need space for their roots to grow, while others need to be staked up for support. They all need the universal nourishment of our love and attention. When we recognize and use our own gifts, we are better able to enrich our students and help them grow.

Sometimes, cultivating the gift of a student may require listening, not talking.

> "I remember Mr. Smith. He was the only teacher who ever listened to me. I felt like what I said mattered. It made me feel validated as a human being, and I began to speak up more often. [Now] I really enjoy getting into discussions and debating things with my friends. I'll never forget him."
>
> —Student

Inside Out

Like the seekers in the Land of Oz who looked to the Wizard for answers, only to find that the gifts they coveted—heart, wisdom, and courage—were already within them, we begin to understand more deeply that *the keys to being a Master Teacher, as well as the keys to happiness, are within us just waiting for our arrival.*

We know from our own experience the importance a teacher can make in the life of a child or young adult. Someone along the way had an impact on us, recognized our gifts, and gave us encouragement. Their legacy lives on in our hearts. We are who we are, in part, because of them.

As pilgrims on the path to Teaching Mastery, we seek to have the same impact on our students, so we keep our hearts open, sensing and supporting their gifts—gifts that hold the key to their deepest passions. It is here, in the realm of gifts, that we can become significant in our students' lives.

> [W]hat we teach will never "take" unless it connects with the inward, living core of our students' lives, with our students' inward teachers.
>
> We can, and do, make education an exclusively outward enterprise, forcing students to memorize and repeat facts without ever appealing to their inner truth—and we get predictable results: many students never want to read a challenging book or think a creative thought once they get out of school. —Parker Palmer, "The Courage to Teach"[2]

You can be the teacher that they remember when they are older—the teacher they thank for encouraging and supporting them.

Giving Gratitude

Mark Twain once remarked, "I can live two months on a good compliment." Yet the good feeling one gets from being on the receiving end of a compliment is only half the story. The person who pays the compliment also feels good. What is most important, however, is that the relationship between the giver and the receiver is strengthened. Gratitude, when given authentically, builds trust, strengthens bonds, and opens the door to relationships. Interestingly, according to research, it also improves health, reduces stress, and in general makes us happier.[3]

Each of us has the ability to cultivate giving and receiving gratitude. It's an emotional muscle that can be strengthened. Maintaining a practice of gratitude is an important element of the personal infrastructure of the Master Teacher. But we should always remember that false praise is easy to spot (especially by our students!). It can actually have the effect of damaging trust and eroding our relationships, so our compliments should be genuine.

Receiving Gratitude

Our ability to feel gratitude that others express to us is directly related to our ability to give authentic gratitude. When someone pays us a positive compliment, do we really allow ourselves to feel it?

Some of us have been taught to be humble and to downplay our accomplishments. But allowing ourselves to receive the authentic feelings of gratitude that someone offers us builds a certain amount of intimacy and trust. Gratitude is the language of the heart. Feeling the inner power of sincere gratitude, from the receiver's point of view, is great preparation and practice for giving gratitude to others. Remember, we work from the inside out.

How often have we deflected compliments with words like "Oh, I was just lucky, I guess"?

Deflecting a compliment is like refusing a gift that someone offers us. It's also a way of shutting down and dissociating from the bodily sensations that get triggered when we're singled out for a bit of praise. Oddly enough, expressions of gratitude can knock us off center as quickly as any disparaging remark. We would do well to recenter ourselves, and simply say, "Thank you" when we receive a compliment.

Deeper Gratitude

Often we think of gratitude merely as an expression of thanks for the good things that we've experienced. But it's also helpful to remember the challenges we've encountered. When we can be thankful, not only for our gifts and blessings, but for the difficulties we've faced, then we've reached a place of deep gratitude. We celebrate the fact that we've survived thus far, that we've used the incident to grow, and that we see the actual progress we've made.

I remember a conversation with a superintendent of schools whom I had coached for several years. He was moving on to a new position, and though we would continue to maintain our personal relationship, my professional engagement with him as the district's leadership consultant was ending.

As I listened to his expression of gratitude for the work we had done together, I sensed how far he'd traveled on his leadership journey. He conveyed his thanks in words something like these:

> "I'm thankful to you, Pete, for turning the 'fix them' conversation we started with to the 'fix *me*' conversation. I wasn't accepting my own accountability back then. I'm grateful for the folks who worked with me over the years who were brave enough to approach me with the truth and hold a mirror to my behavior. I was so self-righteous and had no idea how other people were perceiving me. I'm grateful for the people who cared for me and loved me as I was then and as I am now. I'm thankful for the folks whom I once considered 'enemies' but who were merely following their own paths, on their own journeys. These are the colleagues who presented me with the challenges that helped fuel my own growth."

What a beautiful expression of gratitude! Here was a leader with perspective, one who had transformed his self-righteous, know-it-all attitude into that of a more humble, compassionate, lifelong learner. I had no doubt that he would be successful in his new job (and he was).

It's good to remember that igniting the hearts of our students—by recognizing, supporting, and showing gratitude for their gifts—is where we're most apt to find the true magic and joy of teaching.

REFLECTIONS

1. Gifts are innate, while skills are learned.

2. Our own gifts are always working within us and seeking to surface.

3. Building on our students' strengths both supports and encourages their gifts.

4. To discover our students' gifts, we must first find and use our own.

5. Supporting the gifts of our students ignites their passion and creativity.

6. Recognizing the gifts of our students doesn't have to be time consuming.

7. Expressing gratitude builds trust and relationships.

8. It's important to let ourselves feel the gratitude that is given to us. Deflecting gratitude is like refusing to accept a gift.

9. Gratitude can be cultivated through practice.

10. Gratitude can encompass both good and bad experiences.

ACTIONS

1. What do you believe are your personal gifts and/or strengths? List them. Reflect on your list. Are you using your gifts?

2. Print a roster of your students and next to each record what you think are each student's gifts and strengths.

3. Reflect on what you can do to acknowledge (express gratitude) and support (nourish) the gifts each of them possesses.

4. Maintain a gratitude journal.

5. List some of the difficult challenges you've had to face in your life. Are there things you learned, or feelings you have now, that you're grateful for?

Jody

After the horrors of 9/11, Jody, a middle school art teacher, wanted to expand her students' understanding of the world beyond their own school and their own country. She began using a video-conference system the school owned to connect her students with others around the world. As her students began meeting and exchanging ideas with students in far-off Kenya, they realized that if they worked together they could perhaps tackle world problems—one village at a time.

After much discussion, Jody's students decided to raise money to build a water collection roof and tank system to contain rainwater for a small village in Kenya. Students, teachers, and staff at her school committed to walking and running as much as they could during the month of October. They would keep track of their miles, and sponsors would donate one dollar for every mile they ran.

Teachers designed lesson plans around their global run project. Physical education teachers distributed pedometers, and students tracked the miles. Math teachers had students create graphs for measurement, currency exchanges, and mileage walked. Social studies teachers used the project as a springboard for diversity discussions. Foreign language teachers used it in their classes as a part of a cultural unit. Science and health classes studied the effects that clean (and not so clean) water has on the body and the environment. Jody's own art students created T-shirts and posters to publicize the project.

Within a few weeks, the students began walking the track after school and on weekends. The entire school was buzzing with excitement. They were working together, collaborating on a project much larger than themselves—one that had real meaning. They were motivated, inspired...and learning. In the end, the school raised over $10,000, which was sent to the Kenyan village so it could buy and install its very first water collection system.

The project was so successful, both for the villagers in Kenya and the students at the middle school, that they repeated the project the following year, raising money to build an entire school for the village. This time, however, they were joined by forty additional schools from countries around the world.

Jody remarks of this experience, "When I think about giving, growing, and transforming, I think about an open hand. This open hand both gives and is open to get something back. Whenever you get back, you then have more to give. By living in this way I've been able to grow and transform my life, but also some of the educational thinking in my district."

What a great example this is of how a single teacher, by allowing her heart to shine, can light up an entire school, an entire district, a village in a distant land, and even thousands of students around the world.

CHAPTER 17

CONFLICT

In the midst of movement and chaos, keep stillness inside of you. —Deepak Chopra

I have so much chaos in my life, it's become normal. You become used to it. You have to just relax, calm down, take a deep breath, and try to see how you can make things work rather than complain about how they're wrong. —Tom Welling

Stormy Weather

Whether we're a veteran educator or a rank newcomer to the classroom, it's inevitable that at some point we will experience a wave of feeling overwhelmed, some amount of classroom conflict, and our fair share of disillusionment. These may be brought on by the sheer amount of work we're doing, or the indifference of a few of our students, or a single disruptive child, but whatever the cause, it can leave us feeling frustrated and impotent.

Kate tells the story of her first year as a sixth grade English teacher in the South Bronx:

> It was right after lunch, and I shepherded my class up three flights of stairs and stopped outside my broken maroon door. Before entering I attempted to get my students to line up into "two straight-as-popsicle-sticks, silent lines." I did this every day, because I had read that establishing routines was critical for middle school students. Unfortunately for me, it was always a battle, and on this particular afternoon it took

seven minutes before I let the class enter and begin class.

Immediately, four of my most difficult students took out their "bey-blades," a toy spinning top. These four boys specialized in cursing, crude remarks, and fighting. I thought, "Let them play; at least they'll be quiet."

We had only ten days left until the New York State tests, and I figured it would be better to have the extremely disruptive students silent, rather than battling with them throughout the class. So I let the four disruptive boys play in the back but reminded them that they would be responsible for the same work as the other students.

My "plan" worked for about fifteen minutes, till the four boys began yelling from the back of the room, demanding that I teach them about "deconstructing prompts" as well. I responded by telling them that if they put their bey-blades away they could join the rest of the class. I said this knowing that they'd never put their prized possessions down.

Ignoring the boys only made them angrier, and as I tried to continue teaching my mini-lesson, they began throwing paper-balls and teasing their classmates. After five minutes of nonstop shouting and paper-ball terror, I asked the fifteen students huddled at two tables in the front of the room (who were doing their best to stay out of paper-ball range) to revise their thesis sentences with their partners.

Unfortunately, a handful of previously silent students from the group in front took "group work" as a cue for them to begin shouting back at the four boys acting out in the back of the room. The four boys in the back continued to lob small objects (paper shavings and tiny paper balls) to the front.

The chaos had reached a point that I didn't know what to do. Taking the bey-blades away hadn't worked in the past, nor did threatening detention, nor yelling; so I decided to move the few remaining productive students further to the front, work with them, and ignore the rest of the class.

With five minutes left in class I decided to make a last stand. I knew that the class's next period was their favorite class of the day: physical education. With that in mind, I reminded the class that they had to complete their revisions and submit them to me before they could leave my classroom. Immediately the students began working frantically, trying to complete a twenty-minute assignment in five minutes. A dozen hands went flying into the air to ask for my help; and as I had predicted, only the students who had been quietly working throughout the period finished their assignments.

When the period ended, I opened my broken maroon door to dismiss the handful of students who had finished the assignment. The four boys who'd been sitting in the back of the room bolted for the door. I thought they might do something like this and was ready to block their path by standing with my arms stretched to block their way. They made multiple attempts to escape through my legs and around my arms. When they couldn't get by, they tried shouting at me, telling me how I was jeopardizing their health and they were going to call 9-1-1.

They were holding the rest of the class hostage, and it wasn't long before they all joined in with the boy's cries, "We want to go to gym!" After eight minutes of chaos at the threshold of my broken maroon door, I gave in and let them all leave. They rushed out of my classroom, flew past me, and ran down the hallway, pushing and shouting. As on so many days during my first year of teaching, I was left feeling I should just quit and not come back.

At first I blamed my students for the terrible behavior and chaos in my class. My four problem boys were very disrespectful and mean. I hated to admit it, but I didn't like them. I was doing everything I could to fix the situation, and everything I tried was thrown back in my face. I was really angry and defensive.

Personal Accountability

I know what the problem is, and you're it. —Marilyn Paul[1]

Kate, an inexperienced first-year teacher, let herself descend into anger and blame—a road to nowhere. Why? Because even though she may have been right about her students' disrespectful behavior, nothing she tried changed it. Neither Kate, nor any one of us, has the power to change another human being. Sure, it's our duty to structure and manage our classrooms in ways that facilitate learning and mutual respect; but if a student or several students decide to defy our wishes, they will.

No matter what the consequences, some students will do everything they can to prove to us that they have personal power. They'll do their best to show us that we can't make them learn, or in fact make them do anything they don't want to do. So, other than throwing her hands up in the air in despair, what were Kate's options? Often the best place to start is with a healthy dose of accountability.

Accountability is an emotionally charged word that triggers thoughts of standardized tests, bubbled answer sheets, and days of stress-filled test preparation. It's a term frequently associated with fear, blame, and punishment.

For the purposes of this book, accountability is meant as a personal *awakening to our own power*. It's a recognition that we have the capacity to change ourselves and, by doing so, to change our circumstances. Being accountable is an acknowledgment that we, and we alone, are responsible for our behavior and our lives. It's at once the end of blaming others, a repudiation of victimhood, and a recognition of our innate power. Accountability is one of many difficult steps on the road to Teaching Mastery. For some, like Kate, it is *the* most difficult.

> "After all," we say to ourselves, "I've spent hours developing creative activities and lessons to engage and motivate my students, I've bent over backward to meet them more than halfway, I'm putting my heart and soul into this; but they're still indifferent toward everything I do. They just don't care. They aren't interested in learning. I've done everything I can. It has to be *their* fault."

It's important to recognize that accepting our own accountability for teaching and learning doesn't absolve our students of theirs. It's simply acknowledging that there is no way to force students to learn, or to act exactly the way you'd like them to...unless, perhaps, we're permitted to apply tactics used in the Spanish Inquisition. But apart from boiling our students in oil, we're the ones who will need to initiate new actions and new patterns of behavior.

The End of Victimhood

Kate felt thoroughly convinced that the chaos in her classroom was her students' fault, and that no matter what she did it would fail. Her students would never change. Unconsciously, she had surrendered. She felt like a helpless victim, hoping to survive until the end of the school year.

Kate says:

> One day, as I walked down the hall, I looked in the science classroom and there sat my class from Hell...raising their hands before speaking, paying attention, and behaving properly. I was dumbfounded. I stood there in disbelief. Here

were the same kids who were driving me nuts...acting like model students for another teacher. It struck me that if they behaved for other teachers and not for me, then I needed to change what I was doing. I needed to do something different.

Seeing her students behaving for another teacher was a transformative moment for Kate. Her attitude changed immediately. She began to look even more closely at what she was doing to feed into the chaos. While Kate never fully regained control of her disruptive class, she had learned an important lesson: The power to change her situation did not reside with her students, but with herself. Kate was now no longer a victim.

Getting Out of the Way

To her credit, Kate began the next school year with a clear understanding that she was accountable for creating the classroom learning environment she desired, and she went about making several major changes. Outside of her change in attitude, the biggest was that there would be no more direct teacher-student confrontations, and no more "last stands." Kate realized that she had to remove herself from these types of personal "power" clashes. They were emotional traps that her students would always win.

In the martial art of Aikido, when someone attacks, we step out of the way physically. This allows us to respond without directly engaging the force and energy of the attacker. Once we're out of the way, the immediate threat is reduced, and we're able to control the situation without harming the attacker.

In the classroom, getting out of the way is not a physical move, but a psychological one. In Kate's case, her new move was to take herself out of the picture and acknowledge that, whatever the disruptive student was saying or doing, no matter how hurtful, it was not really about her. She wasn't going to engage it emotionally or take it personally. Getting out of the way made it easier for her to keep calm, return to center, and respond appropriately.

Removing herself from head-on, teacher-student confrontations didn't mean Kate was ignoring bad behavior. Yet she'd learned the hard way that it was much more effective to step aside and avoid slugging it out on a personal level with her students. She took the emotion out of it. No hurt feelings, no anger—just the calm explanation of the rules of the road, and the unemotional and consistent meting out of consequences when the rules weren't followed. When a student acted out, by stepping aside, Kate deescalated the situation, and as her second year progressed her classroom management issues disappeared and her confidence climbed. The pain of her first year had taught her a valuable lesson.

Dominos

A great way to think about "getting out of the way" is to imagine a row of dominos. The first domino is red and represents either our class or a particularly troublesome student. The second domino is blue and represents us. The next domino is red, once again, representing our class, or a student or student(s) within it, followed by another blue domino for us. The pattern continues that way for as far as the eye can see. When we push the red domino, it hits the blue domino, which in turn hits the next red, which hits the next blue, and so on down the line until all the dominos are down.

This red, blue, red, blue pattern can be found in many classrooms. A class or student acts out, and we react. The class, or student, responds to us, and we throw more fuel on the fire by reacting again. One thing leads to another, and soon all the dominos are clicking away as they fall in a familiar and predictable pattern.

Now, imagine the same pattern of red and blue dominos, but this time we've removed all the blue ones that represent us. Now, push the red domino. It simply falls in the empty space left by the blue domino that is no longer there. All the rest of the dominos remain standing intact.

Removing the blue dominos is a reminder that the best way to break a negative pattern is to change our own behavior. When we take ourselves out of the situation (get out of the way), we no longer feed into the old, dysfunctional pattern.

Blending

In addition to getting out of the way, the experienced practitioner of Aikido learns to blend with the aggressor. Physically, it involves stepping aside, then "blending" or "shadowing" (looking in the same direction as our attacker), while feeling the energy, power, and momentum that they're bringing to the situation.

Blending allows us to move without direct conflict. We don't overreact and add fuel to the fire, but we use only the energy and power required for the situation, and nothing more. No one gets hurt. Once again, when we're in the classroom, "blending" isn't a physical move, but instead a psychological one.

When we blend in the classroom, we get out of the way and do our best to see the world from the student's point of view. We aren't minimizing the student's behavior, agreeing with it, or in any way giving in to it. We're still in control, but we're most effective when we remove our own emotion from the situation and have some understanding of what is actually happening from the other's point of view.

Several years ago, I watched in awe as a veteran principal blended with a disgruntled teacher who had been challenging some of the ideas being discussed during his school's staff development program. The teacher was clearly frustrated, and eventually blurted out angrily:

> "I'd like permission to leave. This program is stupid and it's not relevant. I'd rather go back to my classroom and do some lesson planning."

The presenter reacted as if he'd been punched in the stomach, and the entire staff looked stunned. The principal, who was sitting in the back of the room, broke the ensuing silence and spoke in a measured and sincere manner:

> "We're not asking for you to adopt every idea that's presented in the program. But why not give it till the lunch break and see if there might be a few things that you can use to help you?"
>
> The teacher protested, "I've got better things to do with my time."
>
> The principal continued to blend: "You've already brought a lot to the program by challenging some of the ideas [the presenter] has brought forth. I think you surfaced a few thoughts that some in the group may have been thinking about, but weren't willing to verbalize. We need people like you, with different points of view, to be active and vocal so that the learning here is real. The worst thing that could happen is we leave this session and have the real discussion and questions relegated to complaints in the teachers' room."
>
> The principal sat quietly looking at the angry teacher, who was surprised by the principal's openness. His face began to soften and the moment opened in possibility.
>
> The teacher nodded his head and said, "If you think it will help, I'll give it a try."

The veteran principal smiled warmly, saying, "It will. Thanks."

I'd never seen a "blend" like this outside of an Aikido dojo. Interestingly, unbeknownst to him, the side effect of the principal's "blend" was a deepening sense of trust with his entire faculty. After all, he could have taken the teacher on directly and forced him to stay. Instead he handled the situation in a way that maintained the angry teacher's dignity. His staff respected that.

The principal was clearly a Master Teacher.

Winning vs. Blending

Blending doesn't mean we give in to our students or our disgruntled colleagues. If we did, we wouldn't be true to our own center and ground. However, if we simply look to "win," prove that we're right, or dictate the outcome of every situation, then we'll win battles but lose the war. Winning doesn't require understanding, or listening, or blending. When we use our authority and power to win, we talk at our students and colleagues, not to them, and they tune us out.

> When we win it's with small things,
> and the triumph itself makes us small.
> What is extraordinary and eternal
> does not want to be bent by us.
> —Rainer Maria Rilke[2]

We each have the authority and power that comes with being a teacher; but when we "win" by using this power or by managing our students without listening or seeking to understand them, they feel taken for granted and bullied. No one, young or old, likes that feeling. Winning damages respect and destroys the trust so vital to the ecology of effective classrooms.

Jay was approached by a group of students with a list of suggestions for improving his class. At first, he felt insulted, as it seemed like they were criticizing his teaching. He thought, "How dare they!" It triggered a defensive reaction in him. Jay took his work very seriously and spent an enormous amount of time planning what he thought were engaging and interesting lessons. He felt angry.

Fortunately, before Jay responded to the students, he paused, took a deep, conscious breath, and took himself out of the situation. Instead of confronting his students, Jay let them speak. He listened to them as openly as he could. Although Jay didn't commit to any of their suggestions immediately, the students appreciated the fact that he had let them speak, and they seemed pleased that he was taking their suggestions seriously.

It was a classic "blend," and from this place of mutual respect Jay and his students eventually came to an agreement about what was reasonable to implement, and what was not. More importantly, Jay's "blend" opened new lines of communication and new connections with his students while at the same time it sowed powerful seeds of trust.

Too Much, Too Little

Blending relies on feeling what is too much, or too little. If we respond with too much force, the student either becomes defensive and escalates the situation, or withdraws into a passive-aggressive shell. If we react weakly, the student doesn't feel our commitment to them and may push even harder to get our attention. Either way—too much or too little—we increase the chances of doing long-term damage to the relationship and even losing the student permanently.

Relationships are very, very fragile. The whole thing seems

solid, feels solid, is solid. But it can all end in an instant. The more you understand this, the greater delicacy with which you will treat one another and yourself. —Dobson[3]

Like Goldilocks, blending takes getting things "just right." When we're able to "blend," the student is disarmed without using unnecessary force. The relationship may be troubled, but the foundation of respect on which it is built is preserved, and with it the hope for better things down the road.

> I can see my students in a different light and take their be-
> havior less personally. They're just kids, after all. It's near the
> end of the school year, and some of them are excited about
> the birthday party this afternoon. No wonder they don't care
> about the test. If I respond from the FFF [fight, flight, or
> freeze response], I trigger the FFF in my students—which
> does nothing to help them get back on task. If, instead, I use
> my mindful awareness to calm myself and to focus my
> attention, I can work around the distractions and help my
> students stay on task. —Teacher in CARE

Perhaps the Hindu gesture of *namaste* captures the feeling we're trying our best to manifest with our students. Namaste is spoken with a slight bow and hands pressed together, palms touching and fingers pointing upward, thumbs close to the chest. It represents the belief that within each of us there is an authentic self. Namaste is a gesture of acknowledgment by our "true self" of the "true self" in another. We may never actually say the word, or perform the gesture with our students, but namaste is the inner orientation that gives us the best chance to connect and blend with them.

Learning to stay calm amid stressful and chaotic situations, to get out of the way of the attack, and to blend with our students all may sound easy, yet it's not. If we acknowledge that we can never truly control events, or the actions of other people, then we learn to flow with them, and blend, without ever giving up our own power and purpose. As More-hei Ueshiba, founder of Aikido, once said,

> To injure an opponent is to injure yourself. To control aggression without inflicting injury is the Art of Peace.[4]

REFLECTIONS

1. When there is a seemingly intractable problem in your classroom, it's up to you to make an adjustment, and then get out of the way.

2. "Getting out of the way" requires that you clear yourself of negative judgments and differentiate between the students' behavior and the students themselves.

3. Getting out of the way does not mean giving in; rather, it is dealing with the situation in a way that relieves it of high energy and emotion.

4. Blending requires that we are "centered," see the world from the other's point of view, and do our best to find what is too much (or too little) for the situation or the student.

5. When we manage a situation by blending, we allow students to retain their dignity. By preserving their dignity we have a better chance to succeed with them in the long term.

ACTIONS

1. Identify a pattern of behavior you enter into with a student that you think is not effective. How can you adjust your own behavior and "get out of the way"?

2. Identify a student or a class that is not performing as well as you'd like. Brainstorm some ways you might blend with them. Do you need to put more energy into the relationship? Do you need to take a step back from it? (Too much or too little?)

Laura

"Twenty-Five Days to Make a Difference" is a blog authored by an 11-year-old girl named Laura (with the help of her mother). She is a fifth grade student who blogs in memory of her grandfather, who lost his battle with brain cancer. Laura began her blog on December 1st of 2007, doing simple good deeds and writing about them, hoping that she would inspire a handful of others to do the same during the 25 days before Christmas. She wound up with 18,000 visitors to her site in one month, with dozens of people participating, and generated over 800 dollars in charitable donations in just three weeks which she distributed to "good deed doers" around the world. One classroom of winners won a web-conference with two NASA scientists, who donated their time when they saw Laura's site. All of this has been incredibly shocking and rewarding beyond belief. Laura did not expect any of this to happen—she is very new to blogging, but loving every minute of it now. —IZEA blog

---

"Twenty-Five Days to Make a Difference"
Is a Service Project Dedicated to:
My Grandpa, Al Stockman

Albert Stockman was my grandpa. He loved helping other people, and he believed that everybody could make the world a better place, not just by doing big things, but by doing small things too! My grandpa once told me that I was a leader. Even though he called me "Lit-tle Laura," he made me feel big and strong inside.

In 2005, my grandpa got very sick. He was only in his sixties, and he was very happy and healthy before then. I was sad and scared when he was diagnosed with brain cancer. He died only five months later. I was very, very sad when he died, and I felt lonely. My grandpa would not have wanted this, though.

In December of 2007, I decided that the best way to remember my grandpa during the holiday season would be by living my life like he did, by making a difference and being a leader. I decided to honor my grandfather's memory by trying to make a difference every day for twenty-five days. I wanted to be able to do little things, like kids my age typically do, instead of HUGE things that are sometimes hard for kids like me. I decided to write about my adventures here, and I also created a challenge.

I challenged everyone who read my blog to TRY to do something every single day during the holiday season to make a SMALL difference in his or her world. I explained that whoever made the "most difference" in December would win a $25.00 donation to the charity of his or her choice on Christmas night. I SAVED ALL OF MY ALLOWANCE ($25) FOR THE MONTH OF DECEMBER, AND I WAS REALLY SURPRISED AND EXCITED WHEN SEVERAL PEOPLE GENEROUSLY OFFERED TO MATCH MY DONATION (OR MORE)!

RIGHT AFTER THIS FIRST CHALLENGE WAS OVER, I DECIDED TO TRY TO MAKE A DIFFERENCE ALL YEAR ROUND!!

I decided that I wanted to spend 2008 supporting smaller causes in my area that may not get as much attention or support as bigger ones do. I also wanted to pick causes that all of my readers could support as well, even if they lived very far away.

Each new challenge begins on the 1st of each month and ends on the 25th. My family and I use the last week of every month to get ready for the month ahead. I am raising funds for my chosen causes by recycling bottles that people donate to me. I am also doing a lot of service work as well all month long. I work closely with people from these organizations, and I get good ideas from them about how to help them best!

More than anything else, I want YOU to participate.

The individual who makes the most difference for my chosen cause each month will win a $20 donation to ANY CHARITY of his or her own choice!

The classroom, school, group, or organization who makes the most difference for my chosen cause each month will also win a $20 donation to ANY CHARITY of their choosing!

Make sure that you leave a comment or email me so that I know you are participating! If you have a family-friendly blog or website, I will also link back to you so that you get some more visitors!

I hope that this will encourage everyone to make a small difference with me throughout the year!

Love,

Laura

Note: Laura is now 18 years old and a senior in high school. Her blog is www.25xtwentyfivedays.wordpress.com.

CHAPTER 18

BRINGING LEARNING TO LIFE AND LIFE TO LEARNING

It is not what we read but what we remember that makes us learned. It is not what we intend but what we do that makes us useful. And it is not a few faint wishes but a lifelong struggle that makes us valiant. —Henry Ward Beecher

Death Valley

There are days when teaching and learning is dynamic, deep, and exciting. We feel invigorated and fulfilled, and our students seem engaged and passionate. We're on top of the world, and we feel that we're learning as much as our students. But there are also days when we look out at our students and see nothing but emptiness and boredom reflected back. All the lesson planning and preparation, the work that stretched late into the night or through the weekend, doesn't spark a question, a comment, or any sign of interest. We're met with total indifference and left wondering, *is it me, or them?*

On days like this, the classroom terrain can be incredibly inhospitable. It's like standing in the sweltering heat of California's Death Valley gazing at the parched desert floor. Nothing is growing and the terrain seems lifeless. It's a hopeless feeling that leaves us empty, doubting ourselves and even our profession. "These kids don't care about anything," we say to ourselves. "Why put myself through the wringer for nothing?" we wonder.

It's at these desperately lonely moments when the joy of learning has disappeared that we're called to dig deep and persevere. Just when we feel like pulling back, we're asked to give more, because it's during the low points of our classroom lives that we exhibit our true character— that of the Master Teacher. If we can find a way to sustain our commitment, our passion, and our practices during these down times, then slowly, inevitably, things will begin to change. We think,

> "But these kids don't care about learning. They're just here to be with their friends. My classroom's a desert! A lost cause. Nothing can grow here!"

Before we let ourselves fall into despair we should consider the "Death Valley Bloom." In 2005, when the conditions were just right, Death Valley experienced a once-in-a-century wildflower season so spectacular that it made the news all over the country. As if by magic, beautiful wildflowers begin to bloom everywhere, bathing Death Valley in glorious color. Where there was once only dry dust and despair, suddenly there was life. The contrast was amazing.

Not every year will see wildflowers that abundant, yet there are some nice blooms almost annually.

> "This isn't a wasteland. It will start looking empty when the flowers are gone, but there's life there at all times."
> —Pam Muick, Executive Director of the
> California Native Plant Society[1]

The lesson for each of us is that when our classrooms seem lifeless and we get discouraged, there's hope. For just below the surface rest dormant seeds ready to burst into life. It's good to remember this on the bad days in our classrooms...and the good.

Inspiration

How can we bring the seeds hidden within our students' young hearts to life? We can't talk them into germinating, nor can threats of punishment cause them to grow. Using our authority and power merely produces compliance—the minimum response. It's inspiration that produces greatness.

Igniting the power, passion, and curiosity within our students' hearts requires us to cultivate the power, passion, and curiosity of our own heart—and to teach with it, as well.

It's you, the caring teacher, with your unique gifts and the warmth of your heart, who creates the favorable conditions that bring to life the dormant seeds nestled in the hearts of your students. It's you (the "self" you are) that inspires, motivates, encourages, and ignites the fires of curiosity and creativity in them. They will flourish in tapestries of unexpected beauty when they come into contact with your own true heart. That's the magic of teaching.

The way to bring learning to life is to bring your life to learning.

The Power of the Heart

So we return to teaching as "a path with heart." As we've said before, teaching with heart is not a sentimental activity, but simply a way to speak about giving our entire self, body, mind, and spirit to the endeavor. When we teach with heart, we're able to connect to the hearts of our students. Communicating heart to heart gives us the greatest chance to build trust and reach our true potential as educators.

> "A teacher who is attempting to teach without inspiring the pupil with a desire to learn is hammering on cold iron."
> —Horace Mann

If Martin Luther King Jr. had spoken to the crowd with his head rather than his heart when he delivered his famous "I Have a Dream" speech at the Lincoln Memorial, he might have declared, "I Have a Strategic Plan!" Result: Few of the marchers would have returned to their communities inspired to engage in the difficult work of changing the arc of history. Strategic plans are important, for without them dreams can go unfulfilled. But it's only when we combine the logic of our minds with the passion of our hearts and the vision of our dreams that we're able to lead our students to levels of success that they themselves might not believe possible.

I once asked the students in my high school English class to list what they would like to be doing when they finished their schooling. Immediately, they began writing. One student raised his hand and asked,

> "Do you want us to write what we'd really like to be doing—or what we think is realistic?"

I appreciated the young man's honesty, for he reflected a very real sentiment that many of us struggle with internally. While our hearts may have big and audacious goals, we may harbor a secret belief that achieving them isn't possible. Our inner critic tells us, "That's not realistic. It's nothing more than a nice dream" or "You can't do that; it's too difficult!" On and on it goes, until we lose our confidence and a limiting belief becomes lodged in our hearts.

Sometimes it's just the opposite. Our deepest fear isn't that we're inadequate and not up to the task:

> "Our deepest fear is that we are powerful beyond measure.
> It is our light, not our darkness, that frightens us....
>
> "And as we let our light shine, we unconsciously give other people permission to do the same." —Marianne Williamson[2]

The heart is an organ of fire—not one that destroys but one that illuminates the dark. When we organize the thoughts and actions of our mind, body, and heart around our larger purpose, we live from our "sweet spot." We "let our light shine," and it gives others (especially our students) permission to do the same. By liberating ourselves from our fears, we liberate others.

Accessing the power of the heart, and having the courage to speak and act from it, is the stuff of great teachers. It's how we inspire ("breathe life into") our classrooms. It's how we motivate students to do more than the minimum. Inspiration isn't something we can fake. It comes from a deep sense of commitment and purpose, and from summoning the courage to bring a long-hidden and protected part of our self to the surface—our heart.

The voice of our heart is the voice of our authentic and best self. True inspiration, creativity, and passion flow through it, because it represents our deepest values, beliefs, and purpose. When we allow our whole self to become involved in teaching and learning, we become a living, breathing example of a Master Teacher—and learner.

For isn't it true that to become a Master Teacher is to commit ourselves to mastering the art of learning?

REFLECTIONS

1. When we are confronted with student indifference, the way we can bring learning to life is to bring life to learning. We must give more of ourselves, not less.

2. Within every student lie the often-dormant seeds of curiosity and learning.

3. Good teachers teach the mind, while great teachers ignite the heart, as well as the mind.

4. When our actions are aligned with our larger purpose and our hearts are open without fear, we inspire students to achieve far beyond what they thought was possible.

5. Master Teachers are committed to mastering the art of learning.

6. When we speak of the heart, we are speaking of courage and commitment, not false praise, inflated grades, sentimentality, lax discipline, diluted standards, and "feel-good" education.

7. Focusing on the minds and the hearts of our students is not an either-or proposition. We can focus on both.

"If I keep a green bough in my heart,
the singing bird will come."

—CHINESE PROVERB

CHAPTER 19

A Few Thoughts on Practice

We are what we repeatedly do. Excellence, then,
is not an act, but a habit.
—Will Durant

We Are What We Practice

Practice carves a channel, like water over rock. Over time the channel deepens into a gorge and we're able to direct our energy through the new opening we've created to do things that once seemed difficult or impossible to us. Yet while we carve the new channel, and before we're actually competent at the new behavior we're learning, we'll probably feel clumsy and uncomfortable. Unfortunately, this is where many of us stop.

> "People think that the way you make a change is that you wait for it to feel natural or easy. But transformation comes from being willing to be uncomfortable or uncertain. You have to dive right into not knowing. It's hard at first, but the process gets easier over time." —Kelly McGonigal, *Brain Power*[1]

Every time our old friend Principal Ellis (chapter 6) reads the text of his slides to his audience of teachers, he's practicing and reinforcing his old way of doing things. Our daily habits, actions, and behaviors are our "practices." In that context we're always practicing—even when we're not aware of it. In fact, what we practice is who we are.[2]

If Principal Ellis wants to be more effective at his faculty meetings, he'd certainly benefit from practicing a new way of presenting that relies less on simply reading aloud his PowerPoint slides. Our challenge as teachers on the road to mastery is to become more aware of the behaviors that no longer serve us and to practice new ones that will make us more effective in the classroom.

Moving from insight (knowing what to do) to action (doing it) is essential if we want to develop the personal attributes of the Master Teacher. The transition from intellectual understanding to embodied behaviors requires sustained practice. It's important to remember that no matter how clearly we understand which behaviors will be most effective with our students, it's up to us to practice those behaviors often enough that they become a natural part of our classroom presence.

Setting an Intention

We can get more out of our practices if we begin by setting an intention. For example, we could affirm (silently or aloud):

> "As I do this practice today, I want to concentrate on developing flexibility. I believe being able to adapt more quickly to changes in the classroom will make me a more effective teacher."

By stating our intention before we practice, we bring it into sharp focus. We're not just practicing for the sake of practicing but doing it to achieve a concrete goal—for example, flexibility in our teaching methods. Stating our intention before we practice also helps us when our practice starts to become rote and boring, as well as when we get discouraged with our progress. Over time, with repeated practice, our intentions will more closely align with our actions.

Sometimes practicing will feel great; at other times it will feel bad; and, often enough, it will just feel tiresome. This is normal. Practice means we get to try things over and over again, so we'll get a lot of chances to have the practice we want to have.

Coaching

While it's possible to engage in generic and individualized practices by ourselves, having a coach (teacher) can accelerate and deepen our learning by serving as a mirror that reflects back to us certain habits and automatic behaviors that may be difficult for us to see. Much like an athletic coach who notices a hitch in the swing of a golfer, a tendency to overthrow in the delivery of a baseball pitcher, or the improper body position of a basketball player, a coach can travel the path to mastery with us, noticing when our actions aren't consistent with the behaviors we're trying to cultivate—all the while encouraging us to continue the journey.

> Many years ago, I remember meeting at the Red Fox Diner, before work, with Peter, my leadership coach. He pushed a piece of paper across the table and asked me to read the two paragraphs it contained. It was an inspiring statement of purpose: deep, poetic, full of insight and commitment. I was deeply moved.
>
> Peter asked, "Do you know who wrote it?"
>
> I was stumped, and asked, "Who?"
>
> He laughed and replied, "It was you. I had you write this last year when we began working together."

And there it was. I had been so busy focusing on day-to-day issues that I had lost sight of the horizon, my destination—even my purpose. If I had been journeying without a coach, I might never have noticed that I'd lost my way. Peter, though, brought it to my attention at exactly the right time, maximizing the lesson without destroying my confidence and willingness to continue with the journey.

> Whoever enters the Way without a guide will take a hundred years to travel a two-day journey. —Rumi

Partners

For many of us, having a coach isn't possible. Leadership and life coaches are rare in our schools. However, we can get many similar benefits by finding a trusted partner or team of like-minded colleagues who are willing to travel the path to mastery with us. As partners we can practice together, act as mirrors for each other, and serve as wellsprings of emotional support. Receiving specific feedback from people whom we trust, and who are familiar with what we're going through, has a high "nutritional" value—nutrition that will help feed and cultivate our self-awareness as well as the steady growth of our most effective self.

When we decide to practice with partners, one of our first acts is to share our purpose, goals, and intentions. Voicing the behaviors we're trying to embody makes our commitment to practice more real. We can arrange to practice together, or meet to share our progress, our excitement, and our frustrations. Like going to yoga, Zumba, tai chi, the gym, or spin class, if we have friends who practice with us, then the social aspect of our public commitment pushes us to keep practicing even when our initial enthusiasm wanes.

Working with partners has another benefit: it gives us an opportunity to *provide* support, not merely receive it. Partnering enables us to put our learning, our noticing, and growing self-awareness to work for others. Being an active partner and committed listener for someone else even accelerates our own journey. Of course, having a coach who works with us periodically, plus a separate partner who connects with us daily, is the ultimate practice configuration.

Perhaps none of these configurations is possible for us right now. That's okay; the fact that we're considering a commitment to practice suggests that we've already begun the journey. As we continue to walk the path of self-cultivation and mastery, unexpected connections and willing partners are likely to emerge. The important thing is to be present and open to them when they do.

While the journey is deeply personal and unique for each of us, traveling with the help of a coach, a trusted and committed partner, or a small group of like-minded pilgrims will accelerate as well as deepen the process.

Making Time for Practice

For many of us, finding a coach or a practice partner is far from the greatest obstacle to daily practice. The biggest challenge we face is typically finding the time to do it. We're already so stressed and overwhelmed with the demands of teaching that we barely have time to breathe. How on earth can we find time in our crowded schedules to practice?

It's a difficult paradox to accept, but if we happen to be one of the many teachers who are stressed out, feel overwhelmed, and have absolutely no time for practice, then it's even more important for us to make time for it. It's a pretty common mind-set for those who need the benefits of practice the most to feel they're just too busy for it.

Aida is principal of the high school. She explains,

> "I come in to school an hour early every morning to try to get my own work done, but it doesn't take long for someone to show up in my office and from that moment on, the day isn't mine. I'm taking care of other people's problems and putting out fires. My own work just builds up, and I stay later and

later after school to catch up. Where in my day could I possibly find time to practice?"

Aida isn't going to find the time to practice; she's going to have to make the time. She isn't happy when she's given an assignment (practice) to keep a detailed diary—a chronology—of how she spends her time each day for a week.

Later, when she reflects on it, she's surprised to discover how much time she's spending on things that aren't a high priority and could be handled by others on her staff. She also realizes that her open-door policy is being abused by the staff. She decides that closing her door for a few minutes a day won't harm anyone.

Aida agrees to take the first five minutes of the day, before others arrive, to do a brief breath-meditation practice. She also agrees to take five minutes during the time she's supposed to eat lunch (which she rarely does, anyway) to repeat the practice.

Deliberately putting aside ten minutes to practice during the day helped Aida establish a psychological toehold in her stress-filled day. It was the first step in regaining control of her schedule—and her life. The more she made time for practice, the more her narrative began to change from that of a heroic victim, sacrificing herself for her staff, to that of a determined leader who leads change in her building by changing herself.

Making the time to practice was Aida's commitment to turn good intentions into embodied action. It was an act of accountability, as well as a repudiation of victimhood, and it expressed an attitude of "I *can*!" Establishing a ten-minute toehold of self-control in her day was a big step for Aida. It was her way of fighting for herself.

Like Aida, we may need to compromise at first, but making time to practice as often as we can is extremely important. In addition to the benefits of the practice itself, making time for practice is an outward manifestation of our commitment to our journey to mastery.

Without it, sadly, not much will change.

Reflective Practice Modules

While the focus of this book has been on what we can do as individuals to walk the inner path to Teaching Mastery, we would also greatly benefit from implementing what I call Reflective Practice Modules (RPMs). RPMs are structured, professional-development opportunities based on the inside-out approaches to learning that this book describes. Adding RPMs to the traditional mix of workshops, classes, and courses that are generally available to classroom teachers and school leaders would make it much easier for willing educators to begin the inner journey to Teaching Mastery, or to simply improve their overall classroom effectiveness.

Providing RPMs as a standard component of our professional development offerings would create a more formal framework for teachers and school leaders alike to engage in self-reflection, ongoing practice, and constructive feedback. These are all important elements for cultivating a self that builds trust easily, nurtures student relationships, and connects to both the heads and hearts of those we teach and those we lead.

RPMs would equip teachers with powerful tools for self-reflection and self-regulation (that is, mindfulness and centering) and would contribute to reducing rising levels of stress and overwhelm. They would provide a safe place for us teachers to reconnect to our calling and passion, share our stories, speak our own truths. As has been said so many times throughout this book, the focus on cultivating our best "self" results in a deeper appreciation for our calling, a rediscovery and deepening of the joys of teaching, *and* greater levels of student growth—academically, socially, and emotionally.

All this can make the classroom an exciting place where we increase our personal and professional self-awareness, and become better at doing our jobs...and at living our lives.

REFLECTIONS

1. We are what we practice. Our daily habits and patterns of behavior are what we can call our practices.

2. We can learn to embody the attributes of a Master Teacher by engaging in deliberate, sustained practices.

3. Working with a coach or a committed partner helps us to focus and sustain our practices and to accelerate our overall progress.

4. Generic practices set the stage and create the environment for self-awareness and self-cultivation to take root and grow.

5. Individualized practices are specific to each of us and are meant to address unique elements of our own personality.

6. Setting an intention each time we practice intensifies our focus and commitment.

7. We need to make time to practice.

ACTIONS

1. What are your current practices? Make a list. (Remember, we are always practicing. Our habits and behaviors *are* our practices.)

2. Identify a trusted colleague and/or coach who can guide and provide feedback on your practices and can support you on the journey to Teaching Mastery.

The Fun They Had

"...She was thinking about the old schools they had when her grandfather's grandfather was a little boy. All the kids from the whole neighborhood came, laughing and shouting in the schoolyard, sitting together in the schoolroom, going home together at the end of the day. They learned the same things, so they could help one another on the homework and talk about it.

"And the teachers were people....

"The mechanical teacher was flashing on the screen: 'When we add the fractions ½ and ¼....'

"Margie was thinking about how the kids must have loved it in the old days. She was thinking about the fun they had."

—Isaac Asimov

CHAPTER 20

CONCLUSION

*And the end of all our exploring will be to arrive where
we started and to know the place for the first time.*
—T. S. Eliot

No Guarantees

Bringing our best "self" to the classroom doesn't ensure our success. Undoubtedly, we'll encounter students who will refuse to open to us, no matter what we do or how hard we try. The reality is that students must play their own part in the learning process. We can create the conditions for success and open the doorways to learning, but it's they who must take the final steps. We can't do it for them. It can be frustrating and quite sad to see a student suffering, turning away from learning, and yet not be able to help them.

Sometimes the best we can accomplish when dealing with the intractable behavior of a difficult student is to "do no harm." We can only hope that, by maintaining an open heart and respecting the true inner self of the child, we will leave the door open for better things for them in the future. Perhaps we've planted a seed that another teacher will find ways to nurture and bring to life. It may be that, to move forward, the student needs a different environment or a different teacher in a different class.

I wish there were a better answer—some magic tip or technique that we could always count on to work with "difficult" or challenging students. But so far I haven't found it. All we can do, I believe, is to continue to bring our best, most-centered self to the situation.

Classroom Suffering

We all know that K-12 education is undergoing an amazing wave of transformative change. We're empowering students with fresh approaches to pedagogy, implementing innovative curricula that focus on higher-order thinking and problem-solving skills, and equipping our classrooms with powerful new technologies. These initiatives, and others, require us to reorient our classroom practices, familiarize ourselves with new content, and learn new technical skills. As a result, we're spending more time out of the classroom in professional development and training sessions, and more time planning, preparing, and coordinating with our grade level and subject matter colleagues.

All of this change is made even more difficult by the dramatic shift in the makeup of the new students we're welcoming into our classrooms. Increasingly, in schools around the country, we're challenged to meet the needs of new English-language learners, special-needs students, and students from troubled households.

While these transformative changes are happening within the classroom, outside it citizens are engaged in heated political debates about the role of standardized testing, the Common Core curriculum, and the use of big data; whether teachers should be fired if their students perform poorly on achievement tests; whether tenure should be abolished, teacher unions broken, charter schools expanded, teacher certification made more rigorous; and so on.

For classroom teachers on the front lines of educational change, the new content, new pedagogy, new technology, and the increasing numbers of ELL, special needs, and children in poverty, make an already difficult job more stressful, demanding, and demoralizing. These challenges are often combined with noisy political debates, community disengagement, and teacher bashing. It should come as no surprise, then, that teacher burnout is on the increase and the general morale of our teaching corps is suffering.

Today's classrooms don't have to be places of suffering. By redefining Teaching Mastery from "knowledge of content, knowledge of pedagogy, and knowledge of students" to include "*knowledge of self*," we can take care of both the science and the art of teaching. For we must never forget that teaching is a complex enterprise and that learning happens when we teachers and our students connect. Teaching is more than talking, exactly as learning is more than listening. After all, we're not merely teaching content, we're teaching *kids*.

Never has focusing on *the inner life, the emotional well-being, and the classroom "presence" of teachers* been more necessary. There's little doubt that professional development on new curricula, new technology, and new pedagogy is needed to prepare our teachers for the future. Yet we are also called to provide educators with opportunities to explore how they, as human beings, fit into this future.

There is no shortage of "experts" willing to tell educators what to teach and how to teach it. But teachers are already overwhelmed with new mandates and sage advice. My concern is for the caring human beings trying their best to do their jobs in difficult circumstances, and quite often going above and beyond for their students. Teachers need to be honored, not with meaningless platitudes, but by being given the opportunity to explore and cultivate their craft—one that is highly dependent on their personal qualities, their resiliency, and their ability to inspire, motivate, and support our children.

Deeper Meaning

By now, you know that while the focus of this book is Teaching Mastery, it's also meant to serve a larger purpose. It describes the struggles and delights of the human heart surfacing and growing in our lives. It's a journey that each of us takes, in some form or another, during our short time on this earth. The personal infrastructure of the Master Teacher is the personal infrastructure of a meaningful life—"meaningful" in the sense that it is a life lived not only for the self but for a purpose larger than ourselves.

When we're able to tap into our own purpose and passion, we inspire the innate sense of idealism, energy, and creativity that burns perpetually in our students. Then learning becomes relevant to them, and teaching magical to us.

To assist another person on their learning journey is both a precious gift and a delicate matter. We want the footprints on the shore of the ocean of learning to be theirs, not ours. We never want our work as teachers to overwhelm either the answers or the wisdom that each student has within them.

This doesn't mean that each learner must struggle alone. Once again, the Master Teacher battles with a paradox: Students must learn in their own way, and in that sense they are alone. On the other hand, being a teacher who understands that his or her greatest contribution to the learning of students is to gently direct them to their own answers can be an enormous gift.

As learners, we and our students are on the same path. In the darkness, our lantern lights the way and warms the hearts of those who walk with us. If we're lucky, sometimes they even illuminate ours.

This is what makes Teaching Mastery so exciting and so challenging. For Master Teachers don't always trace a straight line. We move as the path, or the updraft of our thermal, or the needs of our students, demand. We must live in the present moment—aware, open, connected to the world around us—otherwise we'll lose our way. We do our best to know the children following us, for if we get too far ahead we'll lose them, and if we move too slowly they'll lose *us*.

> "There is a vitality, a life force, an energy, a quickening, that is translated through you into action, and because there is only one of you in all time, this expression is unique. And if you block it, it will never exist through any other medium and will be lost." —Choreographer Martha Graham

As "teacher," we hold a special place in the lives of the children we see each day. We're the "living curriculum"—a living, breathing, vital example of the possibilities of learning.

Yet we also act as a mirror for our students, one that enables them to see the world, and themselves, anew. It's in this mirror that students awaken to their gifts, their uniqueness, the beauty of their own hearts, and their innate power and strength. It also reflects their blind spots—often hidden in plain sight their entire lives.

We're the cool rain that nourishes the seed. Our true "self"—our open heart—is the energy source that nourishes the classroom landscape. What grows and blooms there is often far beyond our imagining. Rarely do we see the fruits of our labors, but we're deeply grateful and proud to have been called "teacher," and we're at peace with having done our heartfelt best.

Teaching Mastery, at its root, is about paying attention to our students while paying attention to our self. It's about giving everything, though never giving anything that our students aren't ready for or aren't willing to take. The beauty of our journey to Teaching Mastery is that by learning to take care of our self, we've also learned to take care of our students...

...*and* we've ensured that teaching remains "a path with heart."

THE "PERSONAL" INFRASTRUCTURE OF THE MASTER TEACHER

Master Teachers engage in practices that cultivate the following:

1. *Professional and personal self-awareness*
Teaching involves a complex set of knowledge, abilities, and personal attributes in dynamic interplay. By reflecting on the effectiveness of their classroom practices and personal attributes, the Master Teacher seeks to become more professionally and personally self-aware.

2. *A strong connection to their own purpose and calling, as well as a passion for their students' success, their subject matter, and their profession*
Having a strong sense of purpose—as well as a passion for their subject matter, the success of their students, and their own profession—is a prerequisite for Master Teachers to inspire passion, curiosity, and the joy of learning in their students.

3. *A centered presence both while teaching and in the midst of challenging situations*
"Center" is the state of being fully present in the moment (mind, body, and heart), open to possibilities, connected to students (including the mood of the class), as well as aligned with one's own values, purpose, and calling. Master Teachers increase their effectiveness by teaching from center and responding from center in challenging situations

4. *Personal attributes that elicit positive and trusting classroom relationships*
Multiple research studies have shown that positive trust relationships between students and teachers are much stronger predictors of academic gains in elementary and middle school than class size, teacher experience, or the availability of instructional supplies. They are even more significant for at-risk students. Master Teachers deliberately cultivate a self that elicits trust.

5. *Their gifts, attributes, and strengths, as well as those of their students*
Master Teachers develop their personal and professional strengths as well as their own natural gifts. This builds an effective and authentic classroom presence, helps them model lifelong learning for students, and creates a foundation for discovering and supporting their students' gifts.

6. *Resiliency and an ability to break the grip of limiting beliefs, habits, and automatic behaviors that hinder classroom effectiveness*

Master Teachers surface longstanding (and often unconscious) limiting beliefs, historical patterns of behavior, and habitual reactions that limit their classroom effectiveness. At the same time, they work to break their automaticity, allowing them more freedom to make conscious choices in the classroom.

7. *Their ability to manage their commitments without being overwhelmed*

A long list of professional requirements and demands, as well as top-down mandates from state and federal organizations, are major contributors to chronic stress and high levels of teacher burnout. About half the teachers leave the profession in their first five years in the classroom. Master Teachers, by contrast, manage their commitments without being overwhelmed.

8. *An open heart that inspires student passion and curiosity as well as academic and personal growth*

Master Teachers lift students' vision to higher sights, raise their charges' performance to higher standards, and build their personalities beyond their normal limitations. Igniting the power, passion, and curiosity within students' hearts requires Master Teachers to cultivate the power, passion, and curiosity of their own hearts, and then to teach with them, as well.

9. *An awareness of the bodily sensations, moods, and emotions of the "feeling" self*

Master Teachers cultivate an awareness of how their entire "soma" (body, mind, and heart), as well as their beliefs, patterns of behavior, bodily sensations, moods, and gestures, affect student learning.

10. *Their ability to reshape their body into a presence that is aligned with their purpose and goals*

The shape of the body is a mirror of the mind. Leadership, trust, and effective classroom presence all rely on a physical presence that is aligned with the Master Teacher's purpose and goals. If the body is "armored" (muscles contracted and dissociated from feeling uncomfortable sensations), then the Master Teacher's range of physical and emotional action is similarly limited.

Workbook of Practices

Reconnecting to Your Purpose
CHAPTER 4

One creative way to approach reconnecting to your purpose is to engage in an activity called "Giving Ourselves an A."

Imagine that you've finished reading this book and mastered the practices contained within it. You come before an accreditation board that has sent representatives to observe you at work in the classroom and...Congratulations! You've been given the highest possible grade: an A. You're a Master Teacher!

Now, write a letter to the board that begins with the words, "I got my A because...."

Put yourself in the future. Look back and report all the insights you acquired and the milestones you attained on the path to Teaching Mastery, as if those accomplishments were already in the past. Your letter must be written in the past tense.

You can mention the goals you've met, but focus primarily on describing the person you have become. Detail the attitudes, feelings, and classroom demeanor of the person—the Master Teacher—who will have done all they wished to do and become all they wished to become. Fall passionately in love with the person, the Master Teacher, you are describing in your letter.

When you're done, reflect on the letter carefully, for it describes and reveals the Master Teacher that is already within you. It describes your larger purpose and "for the sake of *what*" that you teach.

> "'A' is not an expectation to live up to but a possibility to live into." —Adapted from Rosamund Stone Zander and Benjamin Zander, *The Art of Possibility*

Stating Your Purpose as a Declaration
CHAPTER 4

Writing or stating your purpose in the form of a declaration transforms it from a personal feeling to a powerful statement of intention. Doing so takes it from the private realm of self-reflection into the public domain of action.

Try a declaration format that starts with the words, "I am a commitment to...."

This wording is powerful because it declares that who you are and what you value (your purpose) are the same thing. It says clearly that your actions and your life are aligned with your purpose. This is different from merely having a list of commitments you'd like to fulfill. *Being* the commitment is different than *having* a commitment.

Once you've declared your commitment, you can add your explanations of "for the sake of *what*" that you teach, or why that commitment is important to you.

Here is an example of a simple declaration of purpose:

"I am a commitment to...writing, for the sake of helping educators and students to find professional and academic success as well as personal fulfillment."

Sit-Bones: Awareness Follows Attention

CHAPTER 7

This activity will help you experience the phenomenon of awareness following attention. It's an important exercise, because it allows you to feel firsthand what happens when you deliberately focus your attention. It also is a way to move from the "thinking" self to the "feeling" self, and it gives you a sense of how challenging it is to maintain that focus.

Start by finding a comfortable seat and sitting down. Close your eyes and put your attention on where your bottom ("sit bones") contacts the chair. Do your best to keep your attention focused there, and try not to let your mind wander. Pay attention to what you feel, what you sense. Is there a certain pressure or weight you feel on your sit bones? Perhaps you feel a tingling sensation or a bit of an ache. The chair may feel soft or hard. Remember, your inquiries are first-person, subjective explorations, so there are no "right" or "wrong" answers. What you feel, what you notice, will be unique to you.

Keep focused on your sit bones for a few more moments. Now, you're feeling sensations that you hadn't noticed before you put your attention there. In a mysterious way, your sit bones have come to life! Your awareness of the area has grown. When you focused your attention, an increasing awareness followed.

Now shift your focus to the sounds around you, to see if the principle of awareness following attention holds up. Perhaps you notice the sound of the refrigerator in the kitchen for the first time. As your awareness follows your attention, you may become aware of the sound of two neighbors talking outside, a lawn mower in the distance, or the sound of your own breathing.

Next, shift your focus to your feet. Within seconds you will begin to experience them more fully. You may be able to feel the floor beneath them, the pressure of your socks on your skin, and more.

Each time you focus your attention, without distraction, you will find that you become more aware of things you may have overlooked moments before. Learning to focus your attention is a basic skill for developing "self" awareness.

Mindfulness Breath Meditation

CHAPTER 8

We engage in mindfulness to practice focusing our attention, to be present in the moment, and to bring ourselves back, nonjudgmentally, when we get distracted. When we say "mindfulness helps us to be present in the moment," we mean that we stop thinking about what's coming next, or what's happened in the past, and we can then settle our focused attention on nothing but our breathing.

Mindfulness is one of the most important tools we have to cultivate the "self." Because this practice is so crucial, we do it every day, for a minimum of ten to twenty minutes.

There are many ways to engage in mindfulness. For our purposes, we will provide a simple, yet powerful, basic practice. Commonly, we will perform this practice in a relaxed, sitting position with our eyes closed.

You can start by simply following the physical sensation of your breath as it flows in and out of your body. You can sense it as it enters your nostrils, flows into your belly, and expands your lungs. Then follow your breath as it exhales naturally, and as you do, feel the release and relaxation that comes with it.

Keep your attention on your breath as it enters and exits your body. With each "out breath," let your body settle more deeply into relaxation. On each "in breath," feel the expansion of your chest and shoulders. Notice the pause that follows every in breath and every out breath.

At some point, you may find yourself subtly distracted. Your attention begins to wander, you lose your breath focus, and you begin thinking about something, or even daydreaming. When you become aware of what's happening, notice what you're thinking about, let it go, and gently bring your attention back to the rise and fall of your breath...without judgment.

Loving Kindness Meditation

CHAPTER 8

The Loving Kindness Practice is a variation of the basic breath meditation. Begin by becoming aware of how you're feeling in this moment. Sit quietly, and bring your awareness into your body. If you're not sure what you're feeling, pay attention to the kind of thoughts you're having. Are they anxious? Critical? Self-critical? Joyful? Your thoughts can give you a clue as to how you're feeling. If you're not sure about how you're feeling, see if you can notice how you feel about not being sure about how you feel! Sometimes that makes it clearer.

Now, say to yourself slowly, "Let me be well." Take a breath and say, "Let me be happy." Another breath, and say, "Let me be free from suffering." Let the words drop into your consciousness as if they were stones thrown in a still pond. They will cause a ripple. Repeat the words every few seconds, and after each repetition bring your attention to your emotions. What are you feeling now?

After a few minutes, think about and picture someone who is very close to you and say to them the words "May you be well. May you be happy. May you be free from suffering." As with the first words, let them sink in. Then relax and feel your emotion. As you breathe in and out, repeat these words.

Now, choose a person who is neutral to you, someone whom you neither love nor dislike. Silently say to them the words "May you be well. May you be happy. May you be free from suffering." As in the previous stages of this practice, check in on your emotions and feelings.

Next, choose a person with whom you are angry or having conflict. Silently say to them the words "May you be well. May you be happy. May you be free from suffering."

Finally, think about all living things—each creature, each leaf, each insect, each person on earth. With every breath you take, repeat, "May we be well. May we be happy. May we be free from suffering."

Remember to check in on your feelings and emotions after each repetition.

Emotional Autobiography

An "emotional autobiography" is an expansive résumé of our personal growth—a personal narrative that tells the story of our own life. Our emotional autobiography describes which people and events influenced us along our life's way. It gives us a chance to recognize how those people and events helped shape us into the person we are today. Where did our beliefs about ourself come from? How were our personal tendencies and patterns of behavior formed? What was it, exactly, that we think motivated us to become a teacher? What was it that now has spurred us onto the path toward Teaching Mastery?

An emotional autobiography also provides an opportunity to express gratitude and appreciation for those people and events that influenced us in positive ways, as well as to acknowledge the things that happened that we wish hadn't.

In the context of cultivation of the "self," we use our emotional autobiography as a device to help us self-reflect. If we approach the process with a centered and open heart, it can be a breakthrough to a new level of self-awareness. An emotional autobiography, after all, tells an intimate story. Putting it into words removes it from the shadows and brings it to the world outside ourselves. For some, telling their story is a cathartic event that provides insights into how they got to be who they are today.

I remember one teacher who voluntarily shared her emotional autobiography with a small, trusted group. When she was finished, she said, through tears:

"The story used to 'have' me. Now, I have the *story*."

For this courageous teacher, writing her story broke the emotional grip it had on her.

A contrasting emotional autobiography is that of a young man who described the many challenges he had to overcome growing up. These included protecting his family from the verbal abuse of his alcoholic father, and bringing to light his own courage, kindness, and inner strength (qualities he had never before acknowledged). For him, creating his emotional autobiography pulled back a curtain and allowed him to see the magnificent person that he was, giving him the spark to pursue his dreams.

Try writing a two-to-three-page emotional autobiography. When it's done, spend some time reflecting on what (and whom) you included...and what (and whom) you left out. What else do you notice?

Clearing Negative Assessments

No matter how hard we try, we can't always "love" or even "like" every student we encounter. We're human beings, and we're constantly making assessments and judgments about our students. We can't help it. Sometimes, however, our negative feelings toward certain students prevents us from building the trust and positive relationships we know are so important to learning. The Clearing Negative Assessments practice is one that helps us surface our feelings of negativity and also helps clear them by having us reflect on our own flaws.

Write out each negative assessment you have of the students in a column on the left-hand side of a sheet of paper. Completely disgorge your negative feelings with statements like "He's mean," "She's really disrespectful," and "He's a distraction to others in the class."

After you've finished your list, go to the top of the page and reflect on the negative assessment you've written. Then think back to an incident in your own life when you've exhibited the same negative attribute. For example, you may have written "She's lazy." Remember back to a specific time in your life that you were lazy. For example, maybe you were vacuuming the house and deliberately skipped a room. Once you've remembered a specific incident where you've been "lazy," write on the right-hand side of the page "I've been lazy."

Continue the same process all the way down the page. You may come across a negative assessment that you have difficulty associating with yourself. This is very important. Take some time to reflect, and open yourself to the possibility that you may be missing it. Finding this behavior in yourself is a vital step for building compassion and empathy.

Why is it so important that we link a student behavior that upsets us to our own behavior? It's important because when we realize that we've acted similarly, the realization and thought process that accompanies it humanizes the student and replaces our self-righteousness with compassion and empathy.

Attentive Listening

Let's try an Attentive Listening practice. It's a wonderful way for us to experience what a powerful tool listening can be, as well as just how difficult it really is to do properly.

Choose a partner and sit facing each other. Your partner will be the speaker and you will be the listener. The speaker's role will be to describe one of the most meaningful experiences of their career, while you simply listen.

As the listener you're not to take notes nor to speak. You just listen, without judgments (such as "I can't believe this story is true," "This is boring," "I'd never have said that to somebody," "That's happened to me, too!" and the like). When any distracting thoughts arise, or if you drift off, you are to bring your attention back to the speaker.

You may even want to try to listen without giving any physical responses, such as nodding to the speaker as they speak. You're not to think about what you'll say when they're done, or whether you're doing the practice correctly. Your job is to listen with your full attention.

When the time is up, the speaker debriefs. Did they feel listened to? What was that like? What did they notice about you, the listener? What did they notice about themselves as they spoke?

Then, you, the listener debriefs, summarizing the speaker's story. You describe what you experienced, as a listener, during the exercise. Were you able to keep focused on the speaker? What did you notice about the speaker? What things, if any, threw your attention off?

Trying on Different Shapes
CHAPTER 16

Can the shape of our body affect our mood, emotions, and ability to act? Let's experiment with assuming a few body shapes to find out.

Start by standing with your feet apart, arms at your sides, with your palms facing in toward your thighs. Take as long as you need to center yourself. When you feel fully present, bring your attention to your hands. Keep your awareness on them as you slowly raise them in front of you, and as you do turn your palms upward. What subtle changes to your mood or emotions do you notice?

Go back to your original position. Settle yourself again. Now, round your shoulders forward. Drop your head so your chin is on your chest. How does this shape make you feel? After a few moments, pull your shoulders back while you raise your head to its normal position. Notice the difference in your mood and outlook?

Let's try another shape. While standing, lift your chin so that your head is thrown back. A whole new feeling is present. Return your chin to its familiar position. Feel that?

There are many ways to illustrate the power—sometimes quite subtle—that our body shape has on our mood. Try hardening your eyes by tightening the muscles around them, and staring hard. After a few moments let your eyes soften. A very subtle change in your mood takes place.

It's also like that with your chin and lips. Tighten them as much as you can. Now, let them soften. Feel it?

As you've experienced in these simple exercises, changing our shape, in its many parts, can change our mood, our awareness, and what actions we're able to take to become a more-effective teacher and a better person.

E P I L O G U E S

Mr. Jones

(Chapter 9, "Personal Tendencies and Beliefs")

The teacher with the explosive temper, Mr. Jones, who had a flare-up with his student Marty, began a daily mindfulness practice. After a few months, he was assigned a Loving Kindness Meditation (see Practices section). This meditation started with expressing loving kindness for himself and progressed to expressing loving kindness to those with whom he was in conflict.

Mr. Jones also began engaging in a Clearing Negative Assessment practice (see Practices section). He picked students with whom he was the angriest and wrote his negative assessments of them next to their names. He then described where those same characteristics showed up in his own behavior. In one long passage, he wrote:

> There was one student who'd said and done some things I thought were especially cruel to other students, and even once with me. I listed a lot of negatives about that student, including the word "cruel," and in every case I found similar negatives in my own behavior; but I couldn't bring myself to find a point when I'd been cruel. I was really hung up on this. I was asked to keep reflecting, to relax and not to think about it as much as feel it, and sure enough: the moment I stopped thinking about the word, I remembered a time in fifth grade when I called a girl "ugly and fat" in front of a group of my friends. She ran away crying. Thinking back, what I did was very cruel. I made believe I thought it was funny, but I was deeply sorry for the way I treated her. I was showing off. It was really out of character for me to do something like that.

It struck me like a lightning bolt that I, too, had been cruel. Suddenly, I realized how self-righteous I'd become. I considered myself a step above this particular student of mine whom I'd labeled as cruel because I had never acted as badly as he had—but, in my own way, I had. That was the breaking point. I began to see my students differently. Now I have a little more empathy and patience...and a lot less anger.

Remembering this incident helped Mr. Jones break through his self-righteous assessment of his own "cruel" student. The student still faced consequences for his actions, but Mr. Jones was less angry and a tad more compassionate.

Brian

(Chapter 10, "Resilience")

Brian the worker bee, who had a tendency to overcommit himself (partly because he felt that it was the best way for him to win the approval of others), came to understand that at the root of his tendency was a belief that just being himself was not enough. He believed that he needed to do things to be liked.

Brian was given a "Just Say No!" practice. The purpose of the practice was for him to feel the sensations that streamed through his body when he forced himself to say "No!" to a request. He recruited a partner, whose job it was to role-play by asking him to do things: for example, "Brian, will you serve on our technology committee?"

Brian's practice was to simply say, "No." His partner would ask again, "Hey, Brian, we really need you, and you're so good with technology. You'd add so much to the committee. Are you sure you can't help us?" Once again, Brian was required to say, "No."

Brian noticed that when asked the second time, he felt compelled to give a reason for saying no. "I'm on several committees already," he offered. His partner reminded him to limit his response to just "No," without explanation, and then asked, "Can you serve as an alternate? It wouldn't require much of your time." Brian answered "No" again, then felt terrible. It was extremely hard for him to stick to "No." His partner asked once more, "Could you simply edit the meeting minutes, then? You won't even have to attend the meetings." Each "No" became progressively more difficult for Brian.

At the end of his first practice, he remembers,

> "I felt like I was disappointing everyone, letting people down. I kept wanting to say 'Yes,' or explain why I was saying 'No.' Each time I actually said 'No,' my heart rate jumped and my breathing got shallow. I never realized how strong my compulsion to say 'Yes' was. I realized that I needed to keep repeating the 'Just Say No!' practice.
>
> "I was given an interim strategy to help me break my tendency to please others, and make it easier to say 'No.' Instead of refusing a request outright, I was coached to buy myself some time by saying, 'I can't answer yes or no right now. I have to check my schedule. I'll get back to you within 24 hours.' Having the time to pause and reflect, without having to say 'No' immediately, checked my compulsive tendency. It gave me time to get away from the situation, pause, and respond from my center and not from my automatic, historical tendency. As time went on, I realized that 'Less Is More.' By committing to fewer things, I became less overwhelmed, less stressed, and less taken for granted. I became much happier; and when I did commit to something, I was able to do a much better job."

Francine
(Chapter 10, "Resilience")

A pessimist who believed things would never work out for her, Francine rarely tried anything new with her class because, she thought, "probably wouldn't work anyway." Her eyes were generally cast downward, and she rarely made eye contact with her students.

Francine was asked to write an Emotional Autobiography (see Practices section). An Emotional Autobiography describes which people and what events influenced us along the way. It's a chance for us to reflect on how those events and people have helped shape us into the persons we are today. How were our personal tendencies and patterns of behavior formed? From where did we get our beliefs and values? What was our emotional motivation to become a teacher? And what motivated us to seek out the path to Teaching Mastery?

Francine shared her Emotional Autobiography with a fellow teacher a few weeks later and realized that when she was in first grade her best friend abandoned her and became "best friends" with their neighbor. The two of them wouldn't let Francine in on their relationship or their play. From that point on, Francine felt as though there was something wrong with her:

> "Looking back, I think that I have usually been afraid that if I tried to put myself forward and try to make a new friend, it would end like my first-grade friendship ended. I'd be abandoned again. So I just stopped trying. I think that's where my 'What's the use?' attitude came from."

Once Francine could link her pessimism to its source, she found it easier to adopt a new, more positive belief—one that supported her personally and professionally. "I'm a good person and have a lot to offer, both in and out of the classroom," she practiced saying to herself and even aloud at home, several times each day. Francine's initial attempts at mindfulness and centering practices were full of negative self-criticism. Over time, though, she was able to see how her inner critic, which was sabotaging her attempts at meditation, was also the same harsh critic that undermined her confidence and classroom effectiveness. Within months of concentrating on her practices, her negativity began to dissipate.

Francine also began to work on changing the shape of her body at-rest. Whenever she spoke face to face with anyone, she would take a conscious centering breath and then line up with the person, facing them straight on, while keeping her head up and her eyes focused on the person. She resolved not to hide herself anymore. She reflected:

> "It's amazing that something that happened to me when I was five or six years old has had such an impact on my life! I guess I was really hurt and just retreated into my shell. It feels so good to be out of that shell."

Notes

Introduction

1. New York State Master Teacher Program (NYSMTP), in partnership with The State University of New York and Math for America. www.suny.edu/masterteacher.

Bettye T. Spinner's "Harvest Home" was originally published in the spring 1993 newsletter of the National S.E.E.D. Project on Inclusive Curriculum. © 1998 by Bettye T. Spinner.

Chapter 1: The Inner Path

Carlos Castenada, *The Teachings of Don Juan: A Yaqui Way of Knowledge*, 1st ed., 40th anniversary ed. (University of California Press, 2008).

1. "Increasing the Odds: How Good Policies Can Yield Better Teachers," National Council on Teacher Quality (Oct. 2004).
2. Parker Palmer, *The Courage to Teach: Exploring the Inner Landscape of a Teacher's Life*, 10th anniversary ed. (Jossey-Bass, 2007).
3. The Common Core is a set of high-quality academic standards in mathematics and English language arts/literacy (ELA). These learning goals outline what a student should know and be able to do at the end of each grade. The standards were created to ensure that all students graduate from high school with the skills and knowledge necessary to succeed in college, career, and life, regardless of where they live. Forty-three states, the District of Columbia, four territories, and the Department of Defense Education Activity (DoDEA) have voluntarily adopted the Common Core and are moving forward with it.
4. Richard M. Ingersall, "Is There Really a Teacher Shortage?," University of Pennsylvania, Research Report, cosponsored by the Center for the Study of Teaching and Policy and the Consortium for Policy Research in Education (2003).
5. C.A.R.E., Cultivating Awareness and Resilience in Education, www.care4teachers.org. CARE for Teachers is a unique program designed to help teachers reduce stress and enliven their teaching by promoting awareness, presence, compassion, reflection, and inspiration—the inner resources they need to help students flourish, socially, emotionally, and academically.
6. "The High Cost of Teacher Turnover," The National Commission on Teaching and America's Future (2007), http://nctaf.org/wp-content/uploads/2012/01/NCTAF-Cost-of-Teacher-Turnover-2007-policy-brief.pdf.

"Teachers Wanted: Must Love Students," Keith W. Frome, CEO, College Summit.

Chapter 2: The Power of Relationships

Megan Tschannen-Moran, *Trust Matters* (Jossey-Bass, 2004).

1. Jean A. Baker, Sara Rimm-Kaufman et al., "Contributions of teacher–child relationships to positive school adjustment during elementary school," Michigan State University, *Journal of School Psychology* (2006).
2. Ibid.

3. Ibid.
4. D. Berry and E. O'Connor, "Behavioral risk, teacher–child relationships, and social skill development across middle childhood: A child-by-environment analysis of change," *Journal of Applied Developmental Psychology* 31, no. 1 (2009): 1-14.
5. V. Battistich, E. Schaps, and N. Wilson, "Effects of an elementary school intervention on students' 'connectedness' to school and social adjustment during middle school," *Journal of Primary Prevention* 24, no. 3 (2004): 243-62.
6. Bryk and Schnieder, "Trust in Schools: A Core Resource for Improvement," Russell Sage Foundation (2002).
7. Marilyn Watson and Laura Ecken, *Learning to Trust: Transforming Difficult Elementary Classrooms Through Developmental Discipline* (Jossey-Bass, 2003).
8. Bubois and Silverthorn, "Natural Mentoring Relationships and Adolescent Health: Evidence From a National Study," American Public Health Association (2003); Greenberger, Chen, and Beam, "Negative Adult Influences and the Protective Effects of Role Models: A Study with Urban Adolescents," American Public Health Association (1998); J. E. Rhodes, L. Ebert, and K. Fischer, "Natural Mentors: An Overlooked Resource in the Social Networks of Young, African American Mothers, *American Journal of Community Psychology* 20 (1992): 445-61; Zimmerman, Bingenheimer, and Notaro, "Natural Mentors and Adolescent Resiliency: A Study with Urban Youth," *American Journal of Community Psychology* (2002).
9. S. H. Birch and G. W. Ladd, "The Teacher–Child Relationship and Early School Adjustment," *Journal of School Psychology* 55, no. 1 (1997): 61-79.
10. Birch and Ladd, "The Teacher–Child Relationship" (1997); A. M. Klem and J. P. Connell, "Relationships Matter: Linking Teacher Support to Student Engagement and Achievement," *Journal of School Health* 74, no. 7 (2004): 262-73.
11. Everett Shostrom, *Man, the Manipulator* (Bantam, 1968).
12. Leo Buscaglia, *Love* (Fawcett, 1972).

David Whyte, "Start Close In," from *River Flow: New and Selected Poems*, rev. ed. (Many Rivers Press, 2012), www.davidwhyte.com. Printed with permission from Many Rivers Press, Langley, Wash.

Chapter 3: Cultivating the "Self"

Jack Canfield is an American author and motivational speaker. He is the coauthor of the *Chicken Soup for the Soul* series.

1. Calderhead (1996), Pianta (1999), and Watson (2003), "Five Attitudes of Effective Teachers: Implications for Teacher Training."
2. Ray McNulty, International Center for Educational Leadership Rigor, Relevance and Relationships, *School Administrator* 64, no. 8 (2007): 18-23.

Pete Reilly, "Losers," from *The Teacher's Path*, https://preilly.wordpress.com/2009/03/10/the-professionals-2/

Chapter 4: Waking Up

John O'Donohue and Anam Cara, *A Book of Celtic Wisdom*.

1. Richard Strozzi-Heckler, *Anatomy of Change* (North Atlantic Press, 1997).
2. Patricia A. Jennings, "There Are No Tigers in a Blackboard Jungle," Initiative on

Contemplation and Education Director (June 2011).
3. Linda Hartley, *Wisdom of the Body Moving: An Introduction to Body-Mind Centering* (North Atlantic Press, 1995).
4. David Whyte, *The Opening of Eyes: Songs for Coming Home* (Many Rivers Press, 1987).

William Stafford, "The Way It Is," from *Ask Me: 100 Essential Poems* (Graywolf Press, 1999). © 1998 by the Estate of William Stafford. Reprinted by permission of The Permissions Company, Inc. on behalf of Graywolf Press, Minneapolis, www.graywolfpress.org.

Chapter 5: Reconnecting to Purpose

Lewis Carroll, *Alice's Adventures in Wonderland* and *Through the Looking-Glass*, sub. edition (Norton, 1999).
1. Richard Leider, "For the Sake of What?," from *Being Human at Work*, Richard Strozzi-Heckler ed. (North Atlantic Press, 2003).
2. Robert Frost, "Two Tramps in Mudtime," from *A Further Range* (Henry Holt, 1936).

Pete Reilly, "A Teacher's Story," from *The Teacher's Path*, https://preilly.wordpress.com/2006/12/20/a-teachers-story-conclusion/

Chapter 6: Putting Ideas into Action

Henry David Thoreau, American transcendentalist author.
1. Richard Strozzi-Heckler, *The Leadership Dojo* (Frog Books, 2007).
2. Laura J. Colker, "12 Characteristics of Effective Early Childhood Teachers," National Association for the Education of Young Children (2008).
3. Letitia Usher and Mary Usher, "Nurturing Five Dispositions of Effective Teachers," presented at the 2nd National Symposium on Educator Dispositions (Richmond, Ky., 2003).
4. K. Anders Ericsson, "The Role of Deliberate Practice in the Acquisition of Expert Performance," Florida State University, *Psychological Review* 100, no. 3 (2003): 363–406.

Pete Reilly, "Laird and Bob," from *The Teacher's Path*, https://preilly.wordpress.com/2008/06/18/laird-bishop

Chapter 7: The Practice of "Center"

Lao Tzu, *The Complete Works of Lao Tzu*, Tao Teh Ching and Hau Hu Ching ed., rev ed. (Sevenstar Communications, 1995).
1. C.A.R.E., Cultivating Awareness and Resilience in Education, www.care4teachers.org.
2. Buddhist Meditation, www.wildmind.org
3. Kelly McGonigal, "Brain Power," *Yoga Journal* (Oct. 2012).
4. John Meiklejohn, "Integrating Mindfulness Training into K-12 Education: Fostering the Resilience of Teachers and Students."

Pete Reilly, "The Benefits of Mindfulness."

Chapter 8: Returning to Center

Michel de Montaigne, *How to Live: Or, a Life of Montaigne in One Question and Twenty Attempts at an Answer*, reprint ed. (Other Press, 2011).
1. "Amygdala hijack" is a term coined by Daniel Goleman in *Emotional Intelligence: Why It Can Matter More Than IQ* (1996). Drawing on the work of Joseph E. LeDoux, Goleman uses the term to describe people's emotional responses that are immediate and overwhelming, and are out of measure with the actual stimuli because they have triggered much more significant emotional threats.
2. Morihei Ueshiba, the founder of Aikido.
3. Dr. Patricia A. Jennings, "There Are No Tigers in a Blackboard Jungle," Initiative on Contemplation and Education Director (June 2011).

Portia Nelson, "Autobiography in Five Chapters," from *There's a Hole in My Sidewalk: The Romance of Self-Discovery*. © 1993 by Portia Nelson. Reprinted by permission of Beyond Words/Atria.

Chapter 9: Personal Tendencies and Beliefs

Harley King, *Mother, Don't Lock Me in That Closet!: Selected Haiku, Poems, and Stories*, 1st ed. (Keller University Press, 1989).

David Whyte, "The Journey," from *The House of Belonging* (Many Rivers Press, 1997), www.davidwhyte.com. © Many Rivers Press, Langley, Wash., and printed by permission.

Chapter 10: Resilience

Mary Anne Radmacher, *Honey in Your Heart: Ways to See and Savor the Simple Good Things* (Conari Press, 2012). A writer and artist who conducts workshops on living a full, creative, and balanced life, Radmacher teaches Internet writing seminars and also works with individual clients.
1. Anne Lamont, "Bird by Bird": *Some Instructions on Writing and Life* (Anchor, 1995).
2. Mary Oliver, "The Journey," from *Dreamwork* (Atlantic Monthly Press, 1986).

Pete Reilly, "Tim," from *The Teacher's Path*, https://preilly.wordpress.com/2007/02/23/tim-pickering/

Chapter 11: Present and Connected

Rasheed Ogunlaru, *Soul Trader: Putting the Heart Back into Your Business*, 1st ed. (Kogan Page, 2012).
1. Antoine de Saint Exupery, *The Little Prince* (Harcourt, Brace, 1943).
2. T. Carlson and P. Hastie, "The student social system within sport education," *Journal of Teaching in Physical Education* 16 (1997): 176–95.

Pete Reilly, "Lost at Sea," from *The Teacher's Path*,
https://preilly.wordpress.com/2007/09/17/lost-at-sea/

Chapter 12: The Importance of Trust

Steve Maraboli, *Life, the Truth, and Being Free* (Better Today Publishing).
1. "The Most Effective Teachers Are in a Class of Their Own," Economic and Social Research Council (ESRC), *ScienceDaily* (July 7, 2009).
2. Robert C. Solomon and Fernando Flores, *Building Trust: In Business, Politics, Relationships, and Life* (Oxford University Press, 2003).
3. Richard Strozzi-Heckler, *Holding the Center: Sanctuary in a Time of Confusion* (Frog Books, 1997).

Pete Reilly, "The Power of the Spider," from *The Teacher's Path*,
https://preilly.wordpress.com/2007/05/07/the-power-of-the-spider/

Chapter 13: Building Trust Through Listening

Paul Tillich, *The Essential Tillich* (University of Chicago Press, 1999).
1. Stephen Covey, *The 7 Habits of Highly Effective People: Powerful Lessons in Personal Change*, anniversary ed. (Simon and Schuster, 2013).
2. Greg Mortensen, *Stones Into Schools: Promoting Peace with Books, Not Bombs, in Afghanistan and Pakistan* (Viking Adult Press, 2009).
3. Ralph G. Nichols and Leonard A. Stevens, *Are You Listening?* (McGraw-Hill, 1957).

"A Teacher's Prayer," author unknown.

Chapter 14: Building Trust Through Authenticity

Stephen Covey, *How the Best Leaders Build Trust*, www.leadershipnow.com/CoveyOnTrust.html.
1. Robert F. Hurley, "The Decision to Trust," *Harvard Business Review* (Sept. 2006).
2. Margery Williams, *The Velveteen Rabbit*, reissue ed. (Doubleday, 1958).

David Whyte, excerpt from "Working Together," from *The House of Belonging* (Many Rivers Press, 1996). Written for the presentation of the Collier Trophy to the Boeing Company, marking the introduction of the 777 passenger jet plane.

Chapter 15: Stress and the Body

Esther Hicks, www.abraham-hicks.com/lawofattractionsource/index.php.
1. William W. Deardorff, PhD, "How Does Stress Cause Back Pain?," www.spine-health.com.
2. Fr. Dennis Moorman, "Haiti, Trauma, Spirituality and Somatic Experience," http://maryknollsociety.org/index.php/articles/2-articles/894-trauma-spirituality-and-somatic-experiencing.
3. Richard Stozzi-Heckler, *The Leadership Dojo*, (Frog Books, 2007).

Charles Bukowski, "The Laughing Heart," *Betting on the Muse* (Black Sparrow Press, 1996). © Linda Lee Bukowski. Reprinted by permission of Harper Collins.

Chapter 16: Gifts and Gratitude

Mollie Marti, *Walking with Justice: Uncommon Lessons from One of Life's Greatest Mentors* (Greenleaf Book Group Press, 2012).
1. David Whyte, "Out on the Ocean," from *Songs for Coming Home* (Many Rivers Press, 1989).
2. Parker Palmer, *The Courage to Teach: Exploring the Inner Landscape of a Teacher's Life* (Jossey-Bass, 2007).
3. R. A. Emmons and M. E. McCullough, "Counting blessings versus burdens: Experimental studies of gratitude and subjective well-being," *Journal of Personality and Social Psychology* 84 (2003): 377–89.

Pete Reilly, "Jody," from *The Teacher's Path*, www.preilly.wordpress.org.

Chapter 17: Conflict

Robert Piper, *Mind, Body, Green, 10 Life Changing Tips Inspired by Deepak Chopra* (2010), www.mindbodygreen.com/0-5006/10-Life-Changing-Tips-Inspired-By-Deepak-Chopra.html.
1. Marilyn Paul, "Moving from Blame to Accountability," *The Systems Thinker* 8, no. 1 (Feb. 1997).
2. Rainer Maria Rilke, "When We Win It's with Small Things," from *The Man Watching: Selected Poems,* new ed. (1981).
3. T. Dobson, *It's a Lot Like Dancing: An Aikido Journey* (Frog Press Ltd., 1993).
4. Morehei Ueshiba, "To injure an opponent is to injure yourself."

Pete Reilly, "Laura," from *The Teacher's Path*, https://preilly.wordpress.com/2008/09/14/students-as-teachers/

Chapter 18: Bringing Learning to Life and Life to Learning

Henry Ward Beecher, *The Most Famous Man in America: The Biography of Henry Ward Beecher,* reprint ed. (Applegate, Image, 2007).
1. Pam Muick, Executive Director of the California Native Plant Society, "Death Valley Alive with Flowers," by David Hancock, CBS/AP, Mar. 14, 2005.
2. Marianne Williamson, *A Return to Love: Reflections on the Principles of "A Course in Miracles,"* reissue ed. (HarperOne, 1996).

"If I keep a green bough in my heart the singing bird will come." Chinese proverb.

Chapter 19: A Few Thoughts on Practice

Will Durant, *The Story of Philosophy: The Lives and Opinions of the World's Greatest Philosophers* (CreateSpace Independent Publishing Platform, 2014).
1. Kelly McGonigal, "Brain Power," *Yoga Journal* (Oct. 2011).
2. Richard Strozzi-Heckler, *The Anatomy of Change* (North Atlantic Books, 1997).

Isaac Asimov, excerpt from "The Fun They Had," in *The Best of Isaac Asimov* (Sphere, 1973). Originally published in a children's newspaper in 1951; reprinted in Feb. 1954 issue of *The Magazine of Science Fantasy and Science Fiction.*

Acknowledgments

I've done many things in my life, but none has been as difficult—nor as rewarding—as my years in the classroom teaching English. It was long after leaving the classroom that I came to realize that *who I was*, not just what I taught, had made a significant impact on my students. On visits back to the small Adirondack town where I taught, at speaking engagements with educators around New York State, and through social media and e-mail exchanges over the years, the gratitude of some of my former students has reinforced, over and over again, how significant the personal attributes of a caring teacher can be in the lives of our young.

Of course, I've been blessed to have the most amazing teachers supporting me my entire life: Mrs. Woodruff, my fifth grade teacher who encouraged me to write; Krishna Baldev Vaid, an Indian novelist, writer in residence, and mentor during my college years; and my college basketball coach, Jerry Welsh. I've been nurtured by many others: Dr. John Fraser, Peter Luzmore, Richard Strozzi-Heckler, Thomas White, Mark Mooney, Douglas Firestone Sensei, and Jeanne Denney—world-class leadership consultants, teachers, and friends.

Bonnie Keast was a steady voice who volunteered her time to provide honest and supportive feedback on my first draft of the manuscript. Tom McKeveny, my canoeing buddy, provided the beautiful cover design and the book layout. Mark Woodworth was my talented editor. Each of them provided me with both professional and personal support as I struggled with the learning curve of a first-time author.

I can't help but feel grateful to my mom and dad, who never went to college but who knew the value of a good education, talked about it, and made sure that each of their five children had the opportunity to go on to an institution of higher learning.

Finally, I want to acknowledge the great math teacher and role model I've been married to for more than thirty years. Watching her quietly go about her work day after day is truly inspiring. She cares about her students, believes deeply in her subject matter, and does her best to bring the kindhearted, strong-willed, authentic self I've come to love to each student she teaches.

My wife, Liz Borghard Reilly, is like so many of the talented and committed teachers I've encountered in my life. These are the good people on the front lines, the ones who see up close and deal with our culture's social, demographic, and economic changes. It's these unassuming professionals—folks who never try to grab the spotlight—who humbly and simply perform one of the most important jobs that anyone can do in this world...*teach*.

ABOUT THE AUTHOR

PETE REILLY is coach and mentor to school superintendents, district administrative teams, and classroom teachers. Beginning his career as a high school English teacher, Pete served for many years as the Director of the Lower Hudson Regional Information Center, a consortium of 60 school districts north of NYC, serving more than 250,000 students. He has served as President of the New York State Association of Computers and Technology for Education (NYSCATE), and Chair of the NYS Directors' Committee on Instruction. Pete was recognized as "Outstanding Administrator" by the Lower Hudson Council of School Administrators, and visited China in 1996 on behalf of the United Nations to develop a plan to improve the use of technology in education there.

Pete is well known for his interactive workshops and keynotes and has presented at many national and international educational conferences. He writes extensively on the topic of education and educational leadership and is a recipient of Edublog's Award for Best Newcomer. Pete is a certified Master Somatic Coach and a black belt in Aikido.

Made in the USA
Middletown, DE
22 July 2015